A Bite-Sized P

CW00404492

Will the Tory Party Ever Be the Same?

The Effect of Brexit

Edited by
Paul Davies, John Mair and Neil Fowler

Published by Bite-Sized Books Ltd 2019

Bite-Sized Books Ltd Cleeve Croft, Cleeve Road, Goring RG8 9BJ UK
information@bite-sizedbooks.com
Registered in the UK. Company Registration No: 9395379

Bite-Sized Books Ltd Cleeve Croft, Cleeve Road, Goring RG8 9BJ UK
information@bite-sizedbooks.com
Registered in the UK. Company Registration No: 9395379
ISBN: 9781092449922

Acknowledgements

This book could not be more timely. It has been four months in gestation but comes to the boil just as the Tories take the lid off their own pressure cooker. Their fissures have become open wounds and their second female Prime Minister forced out of office by the 'bastards' as John Major famously labelled them.

The country is in turmoil; Parliament in chaos and the Tories left facing several directions at the same time. Will they survive? Read this and you decide.

This book was Paul Davies' idea. He stuck with it through thick and thin and rejection after rejection; some do not enjoy washing dirty linen in print. That it has reached publication is down to his perseverance. Neil Fowler, as ever, sub-edited it efficiently and quickly. Dean Stockton worked his magic on the cover. John Mair conducted the orchestra from the swamp lands of Guyana and the beaches of Barbados.

Mostly though our thanks go to the authors. None are paid. All are patient. Without them we would no book and no argument.

The Bite-Sized Brexit series will continue with Farmageddon to be published in April. We hope the four books to date have helped the tenor of the debate over Brexit.

Paul Davies, Goring
John Mair, Oxford
Neil Fowler, Northumberland

The Editors

Paul Davies established his own consultancy, after 25 years in the IT industry, focusing on offshoring and outsourcing, initially based on his work in India where he was managing director of a US multinational IT and services company. Having written books on business in India he established Bite-Sized Books, focused initially on business, and then taking in public affairs, lifestyle, children's books and fiction. The books are tagged *the antidote to unread books* – being easy to understand and usually about an hour's read, although some recent books are double that: *Bumper* Bite-Sized Books.

John Mair was born in the then British Guiana (to an 'Old Guianese' mother) in 1950. He went to Sacred Heart RC School in Georgetown. John won the top scholarship in the Common Entrance exam in Guiana in 1961.Then his parents emigrated to the UK. He returns regularly to Guyana.

John has taught journalism at the Universities of Coventry, Kent, Northampton, Brunel, Edinburgh Napier, Guyana and the Communication University of China. He has edited 30 'hackademic' volumes over the last ten years on subjects ranging from trust in television, the health of investigative journalism, reporting the Arab Spring, to three volumes on the Leveson Inquiry. He also created the Coventry Conversations, which attracted 350 media movers and shakers to Coventry University. In a previous life, he was an award-winning producer/director for the BBC, ITV and Channel 4, and a secondary school teacher.

Neil Fowler has been in journalism since graduation, starting life as trainee reporter on the Leicester Mercury. He went on to edit four regional dailies, including The Journal in the north east of England and The Western Mail in Wales. He was then publisher of The Toronto Sun in Canada before returning to the UK to edit Which? magazine. In 2010/11 he was the Guardian Research Fellow at Oxford University's Nuffield College where he investigated the decline and future of regional and local newspapers in the UK. From then until 2016 he helped organise the college's prestigious David Butler media and politics seminars. He remains an associate member of Nuffield. As well as being an occasional contributor to trade magazines he now acts as an adviser to organisations on their management and their external and internal communications and media policies and strategies.

Contents

Foreword

Theresa May is effectively gone. She is a leader in name only

Lord Heseltine

Brexit is the biggest peacetime crisis we have faced and a no-deal Brexit could provoke a national emergency. The depth and scale of the divisions and the narrowness of the majority in favour of leaving the EU mean that the most sensible step would be to put the issue on hold, complete the negotiations and then hold a referendum. Sadly, that option is not available.

But it is in the next phase of negotiations that the details of the UK's future relationship with the EU will be fleshed out.

Depending on what happens in those negotiations, either we will see virtually no change to our current status – in which case, what is the point of leaving? Or, as is much more likely, the Brexiteers will demand significant changes to reflect their own views – views that will appal and frighten much of the electorate when they realise the enormity of what is being done. In essence, Brexiteers want to dismantle much of what we regard as the underpinning of civilised life in the modern world.

A referendum now would at least give people the chance to react to the realisation that the easy and facile promises of three years ago have evaporated. £350m a week for the NHS has become a £39bn severance cost to leave the EU, every penny of it to be borrowed by the current political generation, but to be repaid by the young people coming after them.

I am opposed to all the compromises on offer, from Norway plus to Common Market 2.0 and the so-called Canada-style agreement. In one way or another, they would make us second-class citizens in a second-class country.

MPs have rightly rejected the threat of no deal, which removes one disastrous option. All the other options, half-in half-out, satisfy no one. Only another referendum would give us a chance to stay in and pursue the course we have followed with such success over the past 50 years.

As I told marchers at the demonstration in London on March 23, I dismiss with contempt the image of us as an island wrapped in a Union Jack, glorying in the famous phrase that captured, for so many, Winston Churchill's spirit of defiance in 1940: 'Very well, alone".

I was there. I saw our army evacuated, our cities bombed, our convoys sunk. Churchill did everything in his power to end this isolation. Alone was never Churchill's hope or wish: it was his fear.

Now, I look back over the years: 70 years of peace in Europe, 50 years of partnership between the UK and the rest of the EU. The fascists have gone from Spain and Portugal, the colonels from Greece. Now we have 28 democracies working together on a basis of shared sovereignty, achieving far in excess of what any one of us could individually. Never forget that it was the memories of Europe's war that laid the foundations of the European Union today.

Margaret Thatcher would have been appalled to see Britain excluded from the top table. Theresa May dashed across the Channel in late March, only to be excluded from a meeting of our former partners, and presented with a take-it-or-leave-it offer. That is what the Brexiteers have done to our country: a national humiliation, made in Britain, made by Brexit.

Britain cannot run from today's global realities of a shrinking world menaced by terrorism, international tax avoidance, giant corporations, superpowers, mass migration, the rise of the far right, climate change and a host of other threats.

Against them, our duty is to build on our achievements in the areas of peace and security that the EU has given us, to maintain our trade access where it matters and to keep our place at the centre of the world stage.

We have a responsibility to hand over and pass on to a younger generation a country richer, more powerful and safer than that which we ourselves inherited. And doing so in partnership with Europe is our destiny, not fleeing to a lonely world and the delusion that Donald Trump offers us an easy way out.

The House of Commons is divided and that reflects what is happening in every village, every town and every city of the UK. But MPs can still do their job and many will do it above party loyalty. They will do what they believe is right.

That is all the more their duty now, because Theresa May is effectively gone. She is a leader in name only because she no longer has any control over events. I am sceptical about changing the singer unless you change the song, and a Tory leadership race would be another massive distraction, but we are where we are.

This chapter first appeared as an article in The Guardian.

About the contributor

Lord Heseltine is a former Conservative deputy prime minister.

Future, what future?

Neil Fowler

It has long been said that the battle for Brexit was really nothing else than a battle for heart and future of the Conservative Party. This book may or may not confirm that – as we publish Theresa May has said she will resign if her deal is accepted. History now awaits her.

But what this short publication will show the despair and disdain with which many now view the Conservative Party – while others profess optimism over the future.

Damian Green, once a close confidant of Mrs May, unsurprisingly, is one of those on the optimistic side, move away from recent troubles, once Brexit has been decided, one way or the other.

He says the party should follow one of the points made by a Tory guru form another generation, Keith Joseph, in the 1970s, when he said that instead of the centre ground, politicians should seek the common ground.

"It is a subtle but important difference, in that it means that instead of triangulating between the existing extremes, you identify new areas of concern which the people may have reached before the politicians," says Green. "The Brexit vote showed that there was indeed a disconnect between political conventional wisdom and the desires of the British people. Throughout its history the Conservative Party has been sensitive to such changes, and adept at adapting to them. It needs to do so again."

MP Sir John Redwood has been a thorn in the side of successive Tory leaders on the subject of Europe – and he isn't changing now.

"The misery of our long-running row is likely to continue," he says. European policy has overshadowed his life in the Conservative Party, he says. He would like a change but isn't sure that will happen

"As I write this I cannot tell what the end will be. If Mrs May succeeds in taking us out, without signing the Withdrawal Agreement, the party in the country will be happy and the Conservatives are likely to go up in the polls. If Mrs May ends up delaying Brexit and extending the long arguments over what kind of Brexit and what kind of close future partnership with the EU we should a buy, the misery of the European rows will continue."

Historian Richard Gaunt looks at whether Brexit is the party's Robert Peel moment, as others have often thought, though he believes the comparison isn't strictly accurate.

"The Conservative party's unity has been strained to the limits by Brexit," he writes. "However, comparisons with Peel's repeal of the Corn Laws, which split the party in 1846, reveal important differences between the two episodes. The Conservatives remain in a precarious position, but division is by no means inevitable.

"The perils of divided parties and long periods in opposition are evident to any informed student of British political history, having been experienced by the Conservatives in 1846, the Liberals in 1886 (and 1918), and Labour in 1931.

"On each occasion, the party in question was out of office for a generation and, in the case of the Liberals, never resumed power except as a coalition partner. As a party more than usually defined by its attachment to history, the Conservatives may yet pull back from the brink of a division which is by no means inevitable."

Matthew d'Ancona, a former editor of *The Spectator* and now a columnist for *The Guardian*, says he is proudly centre-right, but Brexit has summoned the very worst demons that lurk in the Tory party's psyche, saying he believes in their values, but the party is becoming repellent.

"I have had it up to here with the Conservative party," he writes. "Not, perhaps, an unusual sentiment to find expressed in *The Guardian*, where this chapter was first published. But, as a centre-right columnist, I do not start from the proposition that all Tories are inherently evil champions of 'neoliberalism' (whatever that means), intent on maximising suffering and despair. I don't express this contempt for the party blithely or to prove a point. This is not an exercise in rhetoric. I mean it."

Another long-standing critic of the Conservative party has been the *Mail on Sunday's* Peter Hitchens In '*The case against the Conservative Party*' he wrote that in 2007 he predicted the end of the Tories. He says his views haven't changed at all.

"Back in 2007 I summed up the case against the Tory Party as it then was. The indictment remains, in many ways, valid."

Financier Victor Hill says he thinks he knows what the Tories are for – but is he deluding himself? He writes that the Conservative Party was an alliance built on four pillars, but those pillars have now moved on – and the Tories haven't.

"What is the Conservative Party for?," he asks. "That is the question that successive generations of Tory leaders have had to confront since the party first emerged as a coherent entity under Sir Robert Peel in the 1840s."

"What has changed us most is the impact of globalism, as much in its digital as industrial forms. This has facilitated the rise of the super-rich, many of whom are trans-national. We mere merchants worry about freedom of capital (relocate to the most efficacious tax haven); and freedom of labour (a tide of economic migrants posing as refugees) – but we know that no one in power is listening."

Journalist Eben Black has been for many years a close observer of all things political and in his *'Game, set and match'* chapter he writes that Tory MPs are not acting like a political party.

"That's why it could all be over for them. The Conservative Party has been at war with itself over Europe since at least May 1940. As the German army rolled through France, we know Winston Churchill and his supporters wanted to fight on with the eventual aim of freeing Europe from the Nazis. Others in the party would have been quite happy to see a negotiated peace and a United Europe under Adolf Hitler, so long as Britain was guaranteed its overseas Empire," he says.

"David Cameron had to go when he lost a referendum called by him and which his arrogance led him to believe he could not lose. The gross misjudgement of calling the referendum was, of course, designed to 'heal' the Conservatives over Europe. Well, you might say, that worked out well, Dave.

"MPs left in the Conservative Party are engaged in vicious battles over Europe, unable to agree on anything despite being in the same party. They are not acting like a party. They are not, any logic says, in the same party.

They cannot all be "Conservatives". It could be that, for the Conservative Party as we know it, it is 'Game, Set and Match', as John Major did not say."

Former editor of The Scotsman, spin-doctor for Ruth Davidson, and now an Edinburgh City councillor, John McLellan says it is Brexit chaos, separation and economic meltdown that keeps Scottish Tories awake at night.

The Conservatives are now the second party in Scotland, he says, and will remain strong, despite Brexit, as voters understand the future of the United Kingdom is the real issue.

"In a country where most economic indicators continue to lag behind the rest of the UK and the burden of taxation is only upwards – higher income tax, higher property transaction tax, and more taxes on tourists and cars on the way – the idea that more of this and breaking up Britain at the same time will somehow make us all better off is what really keeps Scottish Conservatives awake in the middle of the night."

Meanwhile writer Nicholas Stone believes there may be some wilderness years, but the Tories will survive. "Current divisions are not helpful, and previous internal battles were disastrous," he says, "but the Conservative Party will always bounce back.

"The Conservative Party will survive Brexit. Some MPs will defect to new groups, others will compromise their own positions. The disorientating domestic effects of Brexit may lead to a general election defeat and a period in the political wilderness for the Conservatives."

But our concluding writer Liz Gerard does not agree. History will not look kindly on Mrs May," she says, and continues to say.

"The Prime Minister affects the persona of a gawky school prefect with the best of intentions, doing her duty as a vicar's daughter should, a woman so brought up on the path of righteousness that the naughtiest thing she can remember doing is running through a field of wheat," Gerard writes.

"When Mrs May came to power, the nation was smouldering over the Referendum. She could have tried the foam canister, but opted instead for the petrol can. She may yet pull a charred and mangled Brexit out of the fire. But the country and her party will burn for years."

So overall lots of loathing and not too much loving – with a fair dash of pragmatism.

One thing is for sure; this story, so long in the making, is only at its start.

Chapter 1

Occupying the common ground — the best future for the Conservative Party

In a post-Brexit world the Tories must invest as much energy into neglected domestic policies as it has done recently into European affairs, and be willing to change and adapt in many different ways, says Damian Green. If not, the significant problems that face the party, may lead to the beginning of its end

The Parliamentary Conservative Party notoriously has two default settings: complacency or panic. The pressure of the Brexit process has moved the dial significantly towards the latter, although one should never underestimate the capacity of Jeremy Corbyn's leadership skills to encourage Conservatives into the former.

For anyone who thinks long term, though, the departure of colleagues with stinging remarks about destroying the Conservative Party should be worrying. Almost the worst thing about the early days of the Independent Group was that the Labour defectors were clearly distraught about leaving their political home, while the Tory defectors looked exultant.

Is this the beginning of the end? I strongly believe that it need not be, and indeed will not be as long as the post-Brexit Conservative Party pours as much energy into its domestic policies and widening its base as it has into European affairs. Those who are apocalyptic about the party's prospects need to take a step back. In the late 1990s it looked as though Conservatives were destined for extinction in Scotland and Wales. The party now has significant representation in both countries, allowing it once again to become the truly national UK-wide party it has always been.

Also over the last decade the party in Parliament has begun to look much more like modern Britain in all its variety. It seems overwhelmingly likely that, just as the Conservatives were the first party to elect a woman leader, it will be the first party to elect one from a BAME background. Of course there is much more to do but the party has recognised the problem of looking and sounding too narrow and is taking effective steps to address it.

Before I seem to sink back into the mode of complacency I should acknowledge that real problems exist. The membership of the party is not even representative of Conservative voters, let alone the wider country. It is much smaller than it used to be. It is possible to exaggerate how much older the Conservative Party membership is than Labour's, but it is still true that some 44 per cent of Conservative members are over 65, compared with 30 per cent for other parties.

There is also a whiff of intolerance in the air inside the party which is new and dangerous. Deselection is a word which in the past has only been associated with the unpleasant actions of the hard left of the Labour Party. If it becomes a habitual threat from the hard right of the Tory Party it will signify a move away from being a party of government. It should be stamped out immediately.

But to address any of these long-term issues requires progress on Brexit, and then a move on to other matters. We all know that the Brexit vote represented a myriad of discontents, some of them shared across the West since 2008, and some specific to this country. What the Conservative Party needs to do is address the various sources of discontent.

This is more difficult than previously. In 2005, after our third election defeat in a row, I gave the Macmillan Lecture for the Tory Reform Group and observed that "If the Conservative Party does not like modern Britain it is unlikely that modern Britain will warm to the Conservative Party."

Changing political discourse

Much of that problem was solved by David Cameron and his modernisation programme. The current leadership faces the even more intractable problem that modern Britain no longer seems to like itself. The tone of political discourse ranges from the harsh to the disgraceful. Violent language is common. Disgracefully, and occasionally tragically, this spills over into physical violence.

If we are to move on from the current toxic politics the Conservative Party in its post-Brexit phase needs to lead the way, both in tone and content. The tone required is one of respect not just for each other and our varying views but for our political opponents as well. This is not easy.

The current Labour Party is determined to establish a false and unpleasant narrative: that the (necessary) period of austerity after 2008 means that every individual Conservative politician is complicit in creating poverty and misery and is therefore beyond the pale. It is very tempting to respond in kind, but this temptation should be resisted. Raising the debate from the gutter is the right thing to do and will in the long run benefit those who do it, as long as the underlying discontents are addressed at the same time.

Inevitably, after the financial crash of 2008 and subsequent global recession, there are no lack of problems requiring a hard-headed but warm-hearted solution, in the best tradition of One Nation Conservativism. As we move out of the austerity period we have the chance to provide a mixture of targeted increases in public spending and tax cuts which will provide future prosperity both for the country and the party.

That chance will only come if there is a successful Brexit settlement which releases the large amount of stalled investment that has been waiting for certainty, but if and when this happens, the opportunities are huge.

In politics and economics maths is everything. If your economy grows at 2.5 per cent a year, you can afford to increase public spending, cut taxes, and have some left over to reduce long-term debt. If it grows at 1.5 per cent a year, which would probably be our fate if Brexit goes wrong, you don't have enough flexibility.

Although sorting Brexit is therefore the first and overwhelming priority, the choices the party makes in where it concentrates next are key. This is not the place for detailed policy blueprints, but the areas for activity are pretty clear. We need to meet the needs of those parts of the country which did not benefit from the finance-driven globalisation of the 1990s. The Northern Powerhouse was a good idea and needs to be made a reality. Coastal towns, and more generally medium-sized towns with no nearby big city, have special needs.

Clear national challenges

Away from the geographical concentrations of disadvantage which the Government should address, the national challenges are equally clear. The first tentative steps towards a revival of home ownership have been taken, but this ought to be much higher in the political mix. The unfairly neglected Industrial Strategy needs to be at the heart of what the Government both does and talks about between now and 2022. If we get right our policy towards Artificial Intelligence, 5G, electric vehicles, and other new technology, then the effects of Brexit will be relatively small. The same is of course true on the downside.

This is not to neglect the traditional areas of policy dispute. Just as health now has a growing budget and a proper long-term plan, I would like to see education treated in the same way. By education I don't just mean school and universities, but also the FE and apprenticeship sectors, which deserve more attention than ever before.

In social policy, I think grasping the nettle on social care funding should be the start of a much deeper process of rethinking our attitude to the over-60s to recognise the fact that people commonly live to be 90+ and are fitter and healthier than ever before into their 70s. We should stop assuming that everyone over the age of 65 is frail and just wants a quiet life. Staying in the world of work is not just better for the economy, it is usually better for the individual.

There is no shortage of challenges, and happily no shortage of thinking about them. Both my colleagues in Parliament, and centre-right think tanks new and old, are fertile in creating policy ideas. For the country's sake, these ideas need a successful political party to make them real. Far from being defunct, the Conservative Party is needed as much as ever to shape Britain in the post-Brexit world.

Opportunity for all

If it is to meet this challenge, it will need to retain, or in some case regain, its sense of optimism. It is all too easy for Conservatives to become grumpy pessimists. That way lies irrelevance. It also needs to regain the mantle of the party that offers opportunity to all.

The millennials have been foisted with an unfair reputation as entitled snowflakes. They are having to cope with a fast-changing world of work which offers less security than their parents enjoyed, and a significantly more difficult route to settled prosperity in their own home. Most of them want that, and the political prize for offering it is huge. These substantive policy areas will be much more likely to win first-time voters than any improvement to campaigning techniques on social media, necessary though they are.

At the same time, leading Conservatives need to take every chance to show that being a Conservative does not in some way mark you out from the rest of the country. Corbyn's Labour Party is determined to pursue this idea, and it needs refuting. Long ago Rab Butler said he was keen to make it "perfectly possible to be literate, rational, well-informed and a Tory". Today we should be equally keen to make it perfectly possible to be decent, compassionate, outward looking and a Tory.

These various policy suggestions involve recasting some traditional Conservative values, including opportunity for all, home ownership and support for business, to make them fit for the mid-21st century.

They will allow the party to follow one of the wise points made by another Tory guru, Keith Joseph, in the 1970s, when he said that instead of the centre ground, politicians should seek the common ground. It is a subtle but important difference, in that it means that instead of triangulating between the existing extremes, you identify new areas of concern which the people may have reached before the politicians.

The Brexit vote showed that there was indeed a disconnect between political conventional wisdom and the desires of the British people. Throughout its history the Conservative Party has been sensitive to such changes, and adept at adapting to them. It needs to do so again.

About the contributor

Damian Green has been the Conservative MP for Ashford since 1997 and was the First Secretary of State and Minister for the Cabinet Office from June to December 2017.

Chapter 2

The misery of our long-running row is likely to continue

European policy has overshadowed John Redwood's life in the Conservative Party. He would like a change but isn't sure that will happen

My adult life in the Conservative Party has been lived with the long shadow of European Union policy hanging over us.

In the 1970s the Conservative Party was strongly in favour of the Common Market (the EEC) as it then called it. I remember as a young man casting one of my first votes in the 1975 Referendum on whether to stay in. I read the Treaty of Rome which was about so much more than a common market. I decided I was being lied to by those who said it was just a common market with no transfer of sovereignty or loss of the rights of self-government and voted against remaining in the EEC.

During the Thatcher years the EEC evolved towards the comprehensive economic, political and monetary union we know today. As it did so I and others persuaded the Prime Minister that she needed to shift from being a keen advocate of the Common Market to being a sceptic about the wisdom and desirability of monetary and political union for the UK.

This culminated in her Bruges speech and her clear conversion to opposing the single currency and other integration that would follow. Out of office she converted to believing we needed to leave the EU altogether, as it had become something she could no longer support.

In the 1990s the government of John Major was destroyed by his decision to put the UK economy through the torture of the European Exchange Rate Mechanism (the ERM). The adoption of this European policy gave us boom and bust. It undermined the Conservative's hard-won reputation for good economic management and left voters disillusioned by the loss of jobs and the economic damage done to them.

The story line was written by the incoming Labour government, which attributed Conservative unpopularity to the splits in the party over the ERM and over the Maastricht Treaty for monetary union. The polls show a different story. It was the economic damage of the ERM that turned most of the voters off, with a pronounced collapse in support when we were forced out of the mechanism, support which was never recovered.

The public understood the Government had backed a major EU economic policy which had gone horribly wrong, and wished to punish those who had made such a bad misjudgement. The ERM experience forced the Government to lie, with endless statements that the ERM was working and we would never leave it.

The markets knew better and forced us out before more damage was done.

When the Government had to swallow all its words of the ERM era it suffered a breakdown in trust in anything it said. Nicholas Ridley and I were lone voices in government against the ERM fiasco, though I forecast what was likely to happen accurately. Just before joining that ill-fated government I had written a pamphlet explaining how the ERM would lead to boom and bust.

In opposition the Conservatives had a big internal party battle over our attitude towards the Euro. John Major fought to keep open the option of the UK joining before he left office . A succession of leaders in opposition, struggling to regain the Conservative reputation for economic competence, allied with the big majority of the party who were against sacrificing the pound.

I and others made the case that the Euro was the ERM you could not get out of. The Euro, like the ERM, was bound to cause boom and bust, as it duly did for Ireland, Spain, Cyprus and other members.

We pointed out the Euro was always very unpopular with UK voters, who intuitively understood that those who control the money control the management. Leaders found it was possible to unite most MPs and party members around opposition to the Euro and opposition to a succession of centralising EU treaties.

The party voted against acceptance of the Treaties of Nice, Amsterdam and Lisbon. The Labour government sought to mislead the public by claiming these treaties were technical tidying up exercises of little significance. They were instead major transfers of power from the UK and the other member states to the EU. They removed many a veto over particular policies and laws, allowing the EU to emerge as a principal legislator and effective government in many areas of life.

We demonstrated that the party could come together with few dissenters around a platform of opposing more transfers of power to a power-hungry Brussels.

Tories back in power

In 2010 the Conservatives were finally returned to office. The collapse of the economy and damage done to the banking system in 2007-9 was considerably worse than the damage done by the ERM, with a deeper recession. This undermined support for the Labour government that presided over it and gave the Conservatives a chance again.

The problem of Europe however still loomed large. Although by this time there was clear cross-party support for not joining the Euro, the incoming Conservative government found many of its powers had been given away to the EU in treaties we had opposed in opposition.

For many Conservative MPs and party members this was an unacceptable position. Our Parliamentary system rests on the principle that one Parliament cannot bind a future Parliament. A newly-elected government should be able to change some of the laws and policies of its predecessor, because the public has voted them in to change things. In all too many areas this was no longer possible, as the overarching treaties and the cat's cradle of regulations, directives and controls from the EU greatly circumscribed the government's actions.

The Prime Minister was relaxed about the extent of EU control, and tried to tell his party that unfortunately the Treaty of Lisbon had been implemented before he arrived so we could not roll it back.

Many MPs and party members urged him to offer a referendum on whether we should stay in the EU at all, as it was clear to both sides in the argument that the only way the UK could be freed of the Lisbon Treaty was to leave the EU itself.

The argument continued within the parliamentary party until Mr Cameron conceded a referendum promise for the next Conservative manifesto and election campaign. He made this offer at the point where disillusion with his leadership had reached high levels within the parliamentary party.
Eurosceptics demonstrated their growing strength by voting against the government on European matters in large numbers. As the group approached support from half the party the Prime Minister understood the arithmetic and made the concession. He saw off a possible no confidence vote in himself as leader.

Ukip claimed the credit, but my view is the pressure that mattered came from Conservative MPs determined to have a leader who offered a referendum. We also thought it would be popular with the public and would help the Conservatives win an overall majority. The presence of Liberal Democrats in coalition between 2010 and 2015 ensured a more pro-EU stance to government than most Conservatives wanted.

In 2015 the Conservatives won the election, as I and other Eurosceptics thought given the promise of the Referendum. A rather surprised leadership of the party had been preparing for another coalition government, with the Lib Dems exercising a veto over the Referendum plan.

Mr Cameron rightly understood he had to honour this central eye-catching pledge, and undertook the Referendum legislation in good time near the start of the Parliament.

He realised that he would have more chance of winning the vote if he had carried out a successful renegotiation of the UK position. He toured the capitals of the EU member states to see what they would offer to help the UK. He was told they would offer very little. He made very modest requests for improvement, centred around more control of our own benefits system for payments to migrants. He failed to deliver on the issues he had identified and seemed shocked by the very negative response to his 'deal' among Conservative MPs on his return from Brussels.

He and his Chancellor and political adviser George Osborne still assumed Remain would win despite the reversal they suffered in the negotiations with the EU. They refused to countenance any government planning for a Leave win. The Government decided to be very partisan in the Referendum, and helped create the tone of the Remain campaign.

A negative battle

It was remorselessly negative, based around a series of threats and pessimistic forecasts of what would happen if we dared to leave. There was little about why the EU was a good thing, and little about what gains we could make in future from membership. There was a complete denial about political and monetary union. They wished to present the EU as if it were still a grand common market, as if the relentless pressure towards full monetary and political union did not exist.

When they lost the Referendum both the Prime Minister and the Chancellor, who had been such prominent Remain figures, resigned. Mr Cameron broke his promise to send the letter notifying the EU of our intention to depart the day after the vote, beginning an agonising process of delays to the proper pursuit of our exit which came to characterise the next two years and nine months.

The party wanted to elect a Leave supporting MP, but the leadership election failed to produce two candidates for the party in the country to choose between. The parliamentary party chose Mrs May who had been a Remain supporter. A tension grew between the party in the country with very strong support for Leave, and the parliamentary party with a majority of Remain voters. A small number of these Remain MPs did not accept the result of the Referendum and set about using every parliamentary technique to try to delay, water down or even stop Brexit. Three of them eventually left the party to join the new Independent Group of former Labour MPs who also wanted to cancel Brexit.

As I write this I cannot tell what the end will be. If Mrs May succeeds in taking us out, without signing the Withdrawal Agreement, the party in the country will be happy and the Conservatives are likely to go up in the polls. If Mrs May ends up delaying Brexit and extending the long arguments over what kind of Brexit and what kind of close future partnership with the EU we should a buy, the misery of the European rows will continue.

About the contributor

The Rt Hon Sir John Redwood is the Conservative MP for Wokingham, He was formerly Secretary of State for Wales in John Major's Cabinet, and was twice an unsuccessful challenger for the leadership of the Conservative Party in the 1990s. He headed up Margaret Thatcher's Policy Unit and has been a Brexiteer for three decades. He was knighted in the 2019 New Year's Honours list.

Chapter 3

A Robert Peel moment?

The Conservative party's unity has been strained to the limits by Brexit. However, comparisons with Peel's repeal of the Corn Laws, which split the party in 1846, reveal important differences between the two episodes. The Conservatives remain in a precarious position, but division is by no means inevitable, says Richard Gaunt

For Conservatives, there is no more salutary historical lesson of the consequences of leading a divided party than the experience of Sir Robert Peel (1788-1850). Elected with a governing majority of 76 in the General Election of June 1841, the party was split for a generation after Peel insisted on pursuing a policy of free trade, through the repeal of the Corn Laws, five years later.

The party, created in the aftermath of the 1832 Reform Act, divided, with roughly one-third acting as 'Peelites' until the 1860s and the other two-thirds continuing without them. Many leading 'Peelites' joined the newly formed Liberal party after 1859 and the Conservative party did not form another majority government until Benjamin Disraeli's triumph at the General Election of 1874.[1]

A historical parallel?

Superficially, the parallels between Peel's experience and the difficulties facing Theresa May over Brexit are compelling. The Prime Minister faces a (more or less) divided cabinet and party on an issue of fundamental importance which will set the path of national policy for a generation to come. But while Peel argued that he had pursued the most conservative act of his life, by placing country before party, many commentators believe that it will prove impossible for May to deliver on the result of the 2016 EU referendum while retaining the loyalty and support of her party. Indeed, as a result of the pressure applied by different constituencies of opinion within the party, she has already had to concede that she will not lead the Conservatives into the next General Election.[2]

During 2018, Jacob Rees-Mogg explicitly likened May's situation to that of Robert Peel in 1846; however, whilst Brexiteers typically extol historical parallels, they would do well to consider the fundamental differences between the two episodes.

First, Peel's Conservatives were elected to Parliament in June 1841 on a pledge to uphold economic protection, in the face of the Whigs' proposed relaxation of duties on imports including corn. While Peel avoided a personal pledge on the issue, many of his backbenchers regarded it as a betrayal of their electors when he subsequently pursued repeal, in defiance of the platform upon which they had been returned to power. Peel was dismissive of those Conservative backbenchers who fought by-elections to secure a new electoral mandate, after coming out in favour of the measure. For him, sovereignty resided in Parliament, under the clear direction of the executive.

Though there may be comparisons here with the way in which Parliament has asserted its right to be actively involved in the Brexit process, the crucial difference arises from the fact that David Cameron's Conservative manifesto for the 2015 General Election promised a UK-wide referendum on the European issue.

Against all predictions, Cameron secured outright victory at that election and the Referendum was legislated for by Parliament, with large majorities. It was the outcome of the Referendum which entirely transformed the situation. In many respects, Theresa May, who argued to remain in the EU, inherited a situation not of her making. Nevertheless, at the 2017 General Election, May's Conservatives were elected (alongside Jeremy Corbyn's Labour party) on a specific platform to execute the Referendum result by leaving the European Union. Many of the subsequent difficulties faced by the Conservatives have been over how far and in what ways to do so.[3]

Straws in the wind

Peel, by contrast, was moving inexorably towards free trade throughout his 1841-6 government – with many bruising encounters with his backbenchers preceding the final rupture.

For example, during 1844, Peel differed from his backbenchers over a reduction to the sugar duties. The stand-off, which led him to threaten resignation, resulted in the reversal of an adverse vote against his government. The rising Conservative backbencher, William Gladstone, was moved to observe: "it is evident that Peel's mind and the others leaning the same way have been influenced not principally by the difficulties of this individual question, but by disgust with the immense, uncheered [sic], unrelieved labour of their position and with the fact that their party never seems to show energy except when it differs from the leaders". Something of the same spirit was evident in the House of Commons during the 2018 debates over the Withdrawal Agreement and political declaration on the future relationship between the UK and the EU.[4]

In Peel's case, it was the failure of the Irish potato crop in 1845 which precipitated his conclusion that there was no alternative to meet the crisis but full repeal; a diagnosis which many of his 'Protectionist' backbenchers did not agree with. The Duke of Wellington was supposed to have remarked that "Rotten potatoes have done it all. They have put Peel in a damned fright".

However, the direction of government policy, over the preceding five years, had given a clear signal of Peel's ultimate destination. Swathes of duties on imported goods and raw materials and exported manufactured goods had been reduced, especially in the budgets of 1842 and 1845. This had been accompanied by the institution of a 'temporary' Income Tax (payable at seven pence in the pound on salaries above £150 per annum) to help compensate the initial loss in revenue.

Peel's explicit sympathies for changing course may thus be contrasted with May's tendency – at least until the revelation of the so-called Chequers Plan in July 2018 - to keep her powder dry. This was a predicament she had brought upon herself. By failing to secure an enhanced majority in the 2017 General Election, necessary compromises were imposed upon her. She found herself at the head of a minority government, comprised from politically combustible materials, and working with a partner (the Democratic Unionist Party) which represented part of the United Kingdom more than usually impacted by the terms of the Withdrawal Agreement. Her failure to keep them on side may ultimately prove fatal for her government.[5]

I am their leader

Whereas May lost her Foreign Secretary and Brexit Secretary, as a result of pinning her colours to the Chequers mast, Peel initially resigned when he failed to gain the support of his cabinet, after revealing his change of policy to them.

This reveals fundamental differences in their respective positions as leader of the Conservative party. The circumstances surrounding the election of Theresa May as leader in 2016 had ensured that leading Brexiteer candidates fell by the wayside. Though May's path to the premiership was eased, she has subsequently faced continued accusations of lukewarm commitment to Brexit. Her subsequent actions, not least in deferring the critical vote on the Withdrawal Agreement in December 2018, led to a vote of confidence in her leadership which saw her emerge victorious, though with about one-third of her party openly voting against her. This was an ominous figure, in terms of parallels with 1846.

By contrast, Peel was party leader at a time when there was no formal mechanism for election to this position, and he had to use his authority to try and convince his cabinet of the arguments for repeal.

Having resigned in December 1845, he offered his personal support to any incoming ministry committed to repeal. However, Lord John Russell, the leader of the Whig party, failed in his attempt to form an administration and, in Disraeli's immortal phrase, 'passed the poisoned chalice' back to Peel. Newly emboldened, Peel assembled a new cabinet (losing only two ministers in the process). Secure in the belief that he was the only person able to provide good government for Queen Victoria, he now pursued repeal, increasingly heedless of the impact upon his party.

The bitterness within Conservative ranks was given voice by two talented backbenchers, Benjamin Disraeli and Lord George Bentinck, who not only regarded repeal as a betrayal of party but as a slight of honour.[6]

The wider context

Peel was able to pursue repeal, in spite of the reservations of a significant minority within his party, largely because of the supportive votes of the Whig opposition. If May is to succeed in maintaining her fragile hold over the cabinet, and securing backing for her proposals in the House of Commons, she will likewise need to detach some members of the opposition parties to support her. She will also need to secure support in the House of Lords. During 1846, the progress of the Repeal Bill was eased considerably by the leadership of the Duke of Wellington. The Iron Duke allowed Conservative peers to dissent from government policy without imperilling the future strength of the party in the upper house.

However, perhaps the greatest difference between repeal and Brexit lies in the fact that May is not working in a vacuum. Brexit is a negotiation, not only within the cabinet, the Conservative party and both Houses of Parliament, but with the 27 other EU member states, the European Commission and the European Parliament. Whatever unanimity might be achieved in British domestic politics will have been hard won, by comparison with the impressive unity of purpose demonstrated by the UK's negotiating partners.[7]

Historical precedents, current prospects

Though Sir Robert Peel's government enacted repeal, it was defeated immediately afterwards by a combination of 'Protectionist' Conservatives, Whigs, and Irish MPs, who rallied together to defeat the government on a piece of legislation affecting Ireland. The current government's reliance on the DUP for its majority, and the centrality of the Irish border issue to Brexit, means that Ireland is a stronger point of comparison between the situation of Theresa May and Robert Peel than most MPs realise.

The perils of divided parties and long periods in opposition are evident to any informed student of British political history, having been experienced by the Conservatives in 1846, the Liberals in 1886 (and 1918), and Labour in 1931. On each occasion, the party in question was out of office for a generation and, in the case of the Liberals, never resumed power except as a coalition partner. As a party more than usually defined by its attachment to history, the Conservatives may yet pull back from the brink of a division which is by no means inevitable. The sobering reflection for Conservatives must be that none of the promised solutions for the party's 'European Problem' have so far enabled them to do so.[8]

About the Contributor

Dr Richard A. Gaunt is Associate Professor in History at the University of Nottingham and the author of *Sir Robert Peel. The Life and Legacy* (London and New York, 2010). He is currently completing a three-volume edition of contemporary perspectives on the life and political career of Sir Robert Peel. Contact: Department of History, School of Humanities, University Park, Nottingham, NG7 2RD. e-mail: richard.gaunt@nottingham.ac.uk

Notes

1. *See* Richard A. Gaunt*, Sir Robert Peel. The Life and Legacy (London and New York, 2010), chapter 6.*
2. *The Guardian,* 13 December 2018.
3. *Financial Times,* 2 July 2018. Rees-Mogg's intervention came on the anniversary of Peel's death (2 July 1850). Philip Cowling and Dennis Kavanagh, *The British General Election of 2015* (Houndmills, 2016); Philip Cowling and Dennis Kavanagh, *The British General Election of 2017* (Houndmills, 2018).
4. John Brooke and Mary Sorensen, (editors), *The Prime Ministers' Papers: W.E. Gladstone. II: Autobiographical Memoranda* (London, 1972), p.263.
5. For the role of Ireland in British politics, Donal A. Kerr, *Peel, Priests and Politics. Sir Robert Peel's Administration and the Roman Catholic Church in Ireland, 1841-1846* (Oxford, 1982); Jonathan Tonge, Maire Braniff, Thomas Hennessey, James W. McAuley and Sophie Whiting, *The Democratic Unionist Party: From Protest to Power* (Oxford, 2014).
6. For Peel to Cameron, see Charles Clarke, Toby S. James, Tim Bale and Patrick Diamond, (editors), *British Conservative Leaders* (London, 2015); Rosa Prince, *Theresa May: The Enigmatic Prime Minister* (London, 2017).
7. Richard W. Davis, *A Political History of the House of Lords, 1811-1846: From the Regency to Corn Law Repeal* (Stanford, 2007).
8. N.J. Crowson, *The Conservative Party and European Integration since 1945: At the Heart of Europe?* (London, 2006).

Chapter 4

I believe in Tory values, but the party is becoming repellent

Matthew d'Ancona says he is proudly centre-right, but Brexit has summoned the very worst demons that lurk in the Tory party's psyche

I have had it up to here with the Conservative party. Not, perhaps, an unusual sentiment to find expressed in *The Guardian*, where this chapter was first published. But, as a centre-right columnist, I do not start from the proposition that all Tories are inherently evil champions of 'neoliberalism' (whatever that means), intent on maximising suffering and despair. I don't express this contempt for the party blithely or to prove a point. This is not an exercise in rhetoric. I mean it.

By way of explanation: I used to edit *The Spectator*. I am proud to chair a centre-right thinktank, Bright Blue. I wrote a book about the Conservative-led coalition. And if you think that's bad, I was one of the few people in the world who applauded aspects of Theresa May's 2017 manifesto (that's a really select club).

True, I have never been a Conservative member – on the whole, I don't think journalists should join parties, though many excellent ones do so. But, as a believer in fiscal discipline, strong defence, robust anti-terrorism measures, the Atlantic alliance and the social liberalism of those who live in the here and now, I ought to be at ease with modern Conservatism. And I really am not. Brexit has tested that broad affinity to destruction – and in this respect I know that I speak for many on the centre-right.

Yes, Jeremy Corbyn's vacillation has been pathetic. But he is the leader of the Opposition. It was a Conservative government that called the Referendum, and a Conservative prime minister who – having squandered her party's majority in the 2017 general election – bought the support of the Democratic Unionist party with taxpayers' money so she could stay in power and finish the job. Brexit is a Tory gig.

And it has brought out the very, very worst in the party. The attack on 'Teutonic arrogance' – by Mark Francois MP in response to the warning by Airbus boss Tom Enders of the consequences of a no-deal withdrawal – would be easy to dismiss were it not the tip of a nativist iceberg.

It is uniquely dispiriting to see intelligent Conservatives cheerleading or appeasing this drive towards disaster

The very worst demons

Brexit has summoned the very worst demons that lurk in the Conservative psyche, liberating Tories to bellow nonsense about the second world war, the blitz spirit and pseudo-Churchillian defiance. It has fatally compounded the party's demented fixation with immigration and distracted it from the true challenges of the 21st century.

Parliament used to be the crucible of the Conservative ethos: the place where history met contemporary discourse. Now, we have MP Jacob Rees-Mogg – a man still spoken of by supposedly serious colleagues as a leadership contender – urging Theresa May to suspend the legislature if it seeks to thwart a no-deal Brexit.

In the cabinet, we have the trade secretary, Liam Fox, saying that government can be the servant of the people or the servant of Parliament, but it cannot be both. A chilling populism is now creeping into the language of mainstream Toryism: the language of treachery, snarling tribalism and impatience with anything that smacks of prudence, compromise or caution. In the Conservative stockade, emotion has toppled fact.

This, in the end, is the unforgivable act of intellectual surrender. By tradition, the strongest claim the Tories have had to office is a belief that ideology should be subordinated to reality. Even Margaret Thatcher – the most explicitly ideological of Conservative prime ministers – was ousted to stop the Poll Tax and to salvage Britain's relations with Europe.

As Michael Portillo put it a few months after he had lost his seat in 1997: "It is extremely important for the Conservative party to deal with the world as it now is." This was the animating idea behind what became Tory modernisation and the basis of David Cameron's leadership campaign in 2005: the notion that a centre-right party should, on principle, celebrate the diversity of contemporary life and the plurality of modern society. Alas, that project – which reached its high point in Cameron's legislation for marriage equality in 2013 – now lies in ashes.

The whole point of Conservatism is not to submit to the siren call of teleology: the belief that history has an implacable direction. In a crisis of this nature, the proper role of Tories should be to cut through the infantile rhetoric, robotic platitudes and Vogon insistence that "resistance is useless!", and show true statesmanship. Instead, we see – with some outstanding exceptions – a party cravenly fetishising the 2016 Referendum as if no further expression of popular opinion on Brexit were possible; behaving as if the only thing that matters is to get out of the EU by 29 March, regardless of the overwhelming empirical evidence that there is no viable deal, and that a no-deal exit would be a total catastrophe (necessitating, among many other unpleasant measures, a framework for martial law).

Look at them all: fiddling with the backstop while the treaty of Rome burns (or at least the page that bears Edward Heath's signature). It is uniquely dispiriting to see intelligent Conservatives cheerleading or appeasing this drive towards disaster.

Politicians always tell me that the demands of the life are worth it because of the agency you get to exercise. Well, where is that agency right now? Where are the Tories prepared to risk their careers and to say that the instruction given by the electorate in 2016 cannot be delivered in a way that does not do terrible harm to those same voters and their children?

To be clear: I haven't undergone a conversion. My values have not changed. But the Conservative party is morphing into something I find alien and repellent. Like a listing galleon, holed below the waterline, it sails away stubbornly; dragging the nation towards a storm of unknown adversity, peril and pain.

About the contributor

Matthew d'Ancona, former editor of *The Spectator*, is a *Guardian* columnist.

Chapter 5

The case against the Conservative Party

In 2007 Peter Hitchens wrote this blog predicting the end of the Tories. Twelve years on there have been changes in governments, policies and personnel (e.g. Tony Blair and Gordon Brown have left the stage) but he says the overall story and his views basically remain the same...

I give myself a great deal of trouble by attacking the Tories, the party most of my readers want to support. Why do I do this, condemning myself to many angry and often personally rude messages from affronted people? I could easily make everyone happy by quietly dropping this campaign. It would save me hours spent writing letters and e-mails to Tory loyalists who absurdly accuse me, of all people, of wanting to keep Labour in power.

The destruction of the Tory Party, which is now both possible and desirable, is the essential first step to this. In our two-party system, new parties arise out of the collapse and splitting of those they seek to replace. They cannot be created until that collapse, and that split, have begun. A serious, undoubted and decisive defeat for the Tory Party at the next election would make this possible and likely. Such a defeat is possible, despite the events of the past few weeks, and can be aided by voters simply refusing to waste their votes on a party that is both likely to lose, and certain to betray them if it wins.

This view is based on careful study of British voting patterns, constituency boundaries, polls and the age distribution of voters. It is influenced by the experienced pollster Peter Kellner's observation that no opposition party has ever reached power unless at some stage it touched 51 per cent in the opinion polls, during its period out of office. The Tories are still a long way from this figure. In 1979, the Tories were far ahead of Labour in the polls. In 1997, Labour, likewise was far ahead of the Tories. 'Leads' of four per cent, of the kind being achieved now, mean little at general election time.

Even if the Tories could win an election (I speculate on this unlikely event at greater length because so many people now seem to believe that this is the case), what would that mean? I predict a government very similar to that of John Major, only even more torn by its unhealable division over the EU. People forget now, but Major's government was one of political correctness, weakness on crime, failure on education, high taxes and conflict over the EU.

It is claimed that the Tories are now more anti-EU. In truth, this is not really the case. Many Tories have shifted from passive acceptance of the EU to what is called 'Euroscepticism', an unrealistic belief that, while the EU is bad for Britain, it is possible for us to negotiate ourselves a safe corner within it, which does not threaten our independence and laws, or the control of our borders.

This 'in Europe but not run by Europe' view simply doesn't stand up to practical politics. The EU demands of its members a constant and accelerating surrender of national independence. If you win a small battle, you will rapidly find that the EU tries another attack from a different direction to achieve the same end. Don't like the Euro? How about a constitution? The end result, the whittling away of sovereignty, is the same. Why shouldn't it be? Ever-closer union is the EU's stated purpose.

Two honourable positions

In practice, those who are honestly in favour of EU membership and all that it entails, or honestly against it (the only two honourable positions in this debate) still cannot possibly agree – and it cannot be long, in the nature of the EU, before any government is confronted with the choice of continued reduction of national independence, or departure. There is no doubt which option Mr Cameron would choose.

The Tories are also fundamentally, irreconcilably divided over several other issues – grammar schools, the unique privileges due to marriage, political correctness in general, immigration, the size and nature of the state, levels of taxation, the Iraq and Afghan interventions. But Mr Cameron is on the left-wing of all these issues, (including his support for the Iraq war), and so are his most influential colleagues. His authority, were he to win an election, would be similar to that of Mr Blair in 1997, based on the gratitude of a party that had waited too long for office, so his 'right-wing' opponents would not be well-placed to oppose or obstruct him.

It would be the end, for some time, of any opportunity for radical change. It would cement – under a Tory government – the deep leftward shift in this country under Mr Blair and Mr Brown, not least their republican constitutional reforms and their huge increase in the size of the public sector. It would also mean that nothing serious would be done about mass immigration, about education or about crime and disorder.

The restoration of the idea of personal responsibility, and its corollary, punishment for wrongdoing, is not possible in the social democratic state supported by both major parties. This insists that 'offenders' can blame their actions on circumstances, that victims are sometimes at least partly responsible, and sometimes wholly responsible for the crimes committed against them (see police campaigns to get law-abiding citizens to hide their possessions, behave cautiously on the street in case of attracting criminal attention, and fortify their homes).

For those who say that by doing so I help the Left stay in office, I have a simple answer that none has ever rebutted. The result of the next election is already decided – the Left will be in office, either with a Labour majority, or a Lib-Lab pact, or a Lib-Con pact, or a Tory government in thrall to left-wing ideas. No radical change, on the areas which Tory voters care about most, will take place.

I first made this case in October 2003, and I reproduce some of the article I then wrote, all of which still seems to me to be as true now as it was then:

"No power on earth can sustain an idea whose time has gone. Can we all please stop pretending that the Conservative Party is worth saving or keeping, or that it can ever win another election? This delusion is an obstacle to the creation of a proper pro-British movement, neither bigoted nor politically correct, which is the only hope of ending the present one-party state.

The continued existence of the Tory Party as a bogeyman with which to frighten dissenters is one of the few things that holds together the equally bankrupt Labour Party.

Tory division and decay also feed the growth of the Liberal Democrats, whose votes grow daily not because of what they are but because of what they are not. The Tories are an impossible coalition of irreconcilables. No coherent government programme could ever unite them. Euro-enthusiast and Euro-sceptic cannot compromise without betraying their deepest beliefs. Supporters of marriage and supporters of the sexual revolution have no common ground.

Enthusiasts for mass immigration, on the grounds that it expands the workforce, cannot agree with those who fear that such immigration will damage an ancient culture. Those who believe in rehabilitating criminals are bound to fight those who believe in punishing them. Those who wish to legalise narcotics cannot make peace with those who wish to imprison drug-users. All parties are coalitions full of conflicts, but they cannot function without something fundamental that unites them. Nothing unites the Tories.

The wretched Major years, in which Britain experienced its first New Labour government without realising it, are a warning to anyone who imagines that a Tory victory at the next Election would end our national decline or reverse the damage done by Blairism.

The Tory Party is a train wreck, not a train, an obstacle rather than a vehicle. There are many good and intelligent people trapped in the twisted ruins who would flourish if only they were released, but are now prevented from doing so by a pointless discipline."

*

Since then, the Liberal Democrats, it is true, have run into troubles of their own since then – but it is by no means guaranteed that they will not recover between now and the next election. In fact, I think we can pretty much rely on it.

I then redoubled the message in June 2005, when I wrote:

"The haggard patient heaves himself into a sitting position and, with painful slowness, takes a little gruel, swallowing the disgusting pap with difficulty. He, who until recently was consuming rare beef and good red wine, smiles wanly at this minor, toothless triumph. The relatives around the bed exclaim with forced delight how well he has done and how good it is to see him eating heartily again. They make weak jokes and excessively cheerful remarks about how he will soon be home again.

The whole scene is a ghastly, flesh-crawling deception. Everyone present knows that death is hovering a few beds away and there is no hope.

Yet nobody will say it. Such is the position of the Conservative and Unionist Party.

Now, if the Tory Party were a person and we were its family, there would be a good excuse for this polite fraud. But the Tory Party is not a person and we are not its wife and children, or even its friends. There is no point in pretending that the Tory Party is going to recover.

The Tories' position is hopeless. No man living could conceivably unify the party's contradictory wings.

Europhile or Eurosceptic, pro or anti-marriage, market enthusiast or moralist, each of these quarrels is fundamental and cannot be settled by compromise. To refuse to resolve them is to ask to be dragged, by events beyond our control, into places we never decided to go.

What survives of the Tory Party is more like a decayed municipal park than a jungle, and the little furry creatures that roam about in it may have sharp teeth and ready claws but they are not big. To be big, they would at least have to have large ideas. But there are none of these.

The only argument is, ultimately, about tactics. There is a total lack of original thought, principle or even instinct. Every debate is a pathetic variation on one parasitical theme: will the Tory Party regain its position by becoming more like New Labour or less like New Labour?

The answer is that it cannot regain its lost position by either means – because, for good or ill, it has lost it forever in many parts of the country.

Many cities no longer have any Tory councillors. For good reasons and bad, millions of people in large swathes of the country would rather eat a raw hedgehog sandwich than vote Conservative again. A male under the age of 35 is as likely to support the Tories as he is to smoke a pipe. A female under the age of 35 is as likely to support the Tories as she is to wear a girdle.

And here is the core of it. The Tory Party does not know what it is supposed to be opposing. In fact, in general, it has either supported or failed to oppose all the most important actions of New Labour.

Millions long for a truly Nasty government that will be thoroughly horrid to the wicked, the criminal, the dishonest and to the European Union. But to be Nasty, without meaning to, is worse than useless.

And to be Nice about these things is to let down the besieged, oppressed, vandalised, burgled, mugged people of Britain.

It is surely possible to find a majority out there for a new party, neither bigoted nor politically correct, patriotic and intelligent, committed to national independence and liberty and to the re-establishment of justice. I believe those conservatives willing to think, and to seek allies, could swiftly develop a programme and a coalition far more honourable and realistic than the present Tory impasse.

We cannot go on avoiding this decision forever. There will not be many more chances to wrest Britain from the 'progressive consensus'.

Tories are dying and not being replaced. The party is becoming what marketing men call a 'ghost brand', like Capstan Full Strength cigarettes: still worth selling to a dwindling market but with no hope of regaining its lost position.

*

Again, I think this stands up pretty well. Note that, at that point, David Cameron was not a serious contender for the leadership. But my words – "As for the other compromise candidates being spoken of, they all offer another period of Majorism, neither one damned thing nor the other, yet encouraging bitter divisions by attempting to impose their opaque blandness on all" – seem to me to be pretty close to a prophecy of Mr Cameron's behaviour.

Why the Tories must go

There, now I have set it all out, as clearly as I can. Those who absurdly accuse me of seeking to help New Labour or of supporting Mr Brown should know that I am probably the most consistent and dedicated foe of New Labour, that my 1999 book *'The Abolition of Britain'* was described by Andrew Marr (no less) as the "most sustained, internally logical and powerful attack on Tony Blair and all his works", that I refused to toady to Anthony Blair when many other conservative commentators were doing so, that I criticised Mr Brown's bad stewardship of the economy, when many Conservatives were praising him and that New Labour blame me (exaggeratedly, but flatteringly) for helping to lose them the 1992 election (the *'Jennifer's Ear'* affair) and regard me (accurately) as a dedicated enemy.

It is precisely because I really do want to get rid of New Labour that I am convinced that the Tories must go. They don't really want to fight New Labour, and they are not specially angered or dismayed by the way in which New Labour runs the country. Given the opportunity, they would do little that was different.

I think voting is a political act designed to have a practical effect, not an emotional spasm to make myself feel better. Withdrawing your vote from the Tories is the only serious opportunity you have to make the country better. Anyone who responds to this by saying "That's all very well, but the important thing is to get New Labour out" will be showing that they haven't read, or understood, what I am saying here.

Anyone who says "why don't you found your new party?' has likewise not been paying attention. The new party can only be founded once the Tories have collapsed – and you will have to found it too.

If I wait long enough, I am sure that my view on the Tory Party will become conventional wisdom, as most of my other 'outrageous' and 'extremist' positions have done in the last ten years. But can we afford to wait that long?

About the contributor

Peter Hitchens is a journalist and author. He writes for *The Mail on Sunday* and is a former foreign correspondent in Moscow and Washington. He has published eight books.

Chapter 6

I think I know what the Tories are for – but am I deluding myself?

The Conservative Party was an alliance built on four pillars, says Victor Hill, but those pillars have now moved on – and the Tories haven't

What is the Conservative Party for? That is the question that successive generations of Tory leaders have had to confront since the party first emerged as a coherent entity under Sir Robert Peel in the 1840s. That was in the aftermath of the Great Reform Act of 1832 which expanded suffrage for the first time and the internecine animosity precipitated by the repeal of the Corn Laws.

From the first, the Conservative Party was an alliance of mutual interests between very different social groups. The aristocracy, inspired by a past that made them landed, joined forces with the merchant class who foresaw a moneyed future. Together, they could propel the economic and social changes demanded by the coming of the railways, the emergence of (what we would call) consumerism, the displacement of populations from the countryside to the towns...the rise of Empire...

A fragile alliance

In time, the ranks of the merchant classes were swelled by what Lenin called *the aristocracy of labour* – the aspirant, upwardly-mobile section of the working classes who gained property as the 19th century proceeded. Disraeli expanded the franchise to include these people. Mrs Thatcher specifically reached out to them much later with her notions of *property-owning democracy* and *popular capitalism*.

This sometimes fragile alliance always rested on at least four pillars.

The first was the prosperity of the nation – what we would call *the economy*. Conservatives have always believed that wealth is generated by private businesses rather than by state-sponsored investment. Very few people (except Marxists) talked about *capitalism* in the 19th century – most successful capitalists sought to become faux aristocrats.

Capitalists only came to describe themselves as capitalists much later. Long before his controversial (or infamous – depending on your point of view) *Rivers of blood* speech in 1968, Enoch Powell, in one of his essays, wrote that the Conservative Party was the party of capitalism. "When I think of millionaires, wrote Powell, "I smile."

Even today, few British millionaires describe themselves as *capitalists*. But the notion that people should be allowed, even encouraged, to take risks by setting up businesses and thereby generating wealth is supported by virtually all Tory voters, and not just rich ones. The corollary to that is that, while virtually all Tories recognise that the state needs to harvest a judicious amount of tax to finance social goods, taxes should not be so high as to impede private business. Tories aspire to *low taxes* (though just how much spending is appropriate is a much more nuanced problem).

The second pillar was love of nation – and increasingly the British nation rather than just the English one. This has manifested itself in various forms over time – patriotism, nationalism, imperialism. This is not the place to define how each of those concepts differ. Patriotism is now socially acceptable (just); but nationalism is generally considered obnoxious (unless it is Scottish, Welsh or Irish nationalism in which case it must be respected). Imperialism, according to the prevailing orthodoxy, was a historic crime – one for which reparations are still pending...

Of course, the Tories never had a monopoly on patriotism. White working class Labour voters were also self-proclaimed patriots – until quite recently. But the Tories took pride in a nation that stood tall amongst others, had strong armed forces and a prestigious monarchy.

The third pillar was an aspiration to social betterment. Disraeli decreed that the aim of the party was *the amelioration of the condition of the people*. This implies a high value being placed on education, including self-education. The School Boards of the 1860s were strongly supported by the Tories, as was the ground-breaking Education Act of 1944. Tories have tended to assume that people are born with unequal talents and that those with specific talents should be nurtured accordingly. They deeply resent the Socialist notion that everyone should be treated the same because they *are* the same. Tories are deeply attached to the idea of social mobility – that is why no true Tory is a snob.

Of course life is unfair – or so Tories have believed. At the same time there should be a safety net for those at the bottom end. Over the last 175 years Tories have increasingly acquiesced in more state intervention to support the less fortunate – successively giving full backing to the welfare state and the National Health Service. Though some of us (we are sometimes derided as reactionaries) have questioned just how much of the national cake the welfare state and the NHS should consume.

We have obviously moved well beyond Lord Beveridge's *safety net* – into a realm where some people spend their entire lives on one form of welfare or another. (Housing benefit alone now costs more than the Royal Navy). Modern Conservatives have found it very difficult to have this conversation – possibly for fear of being demonised by prevailing leftist orthodoxy on welfare economics.

The fourth pillar was always freedom – interpreted in a very British sense of that idea. People are individuals under the law before they are citizens. The state has no business telling people what to do unless it has very good reason to do so.

This strain of individualism has always been in tension with a strain of social conservatism which has always been present in the Tory psyche – sometimes with bizarre results. Apparently, many Tories thought the state had the right to determine what consenting adults do in the privacy of their bedrooms even after 1968.

A demoted power

Britain emerged from WWII in 1945 as a demoted power – but that did not become fully apparent until 1956. Thereafter, the British Empire was dismantled in a kind of closing-down sale. (Even nations, like Malta, which petitioned to become an integral part of the UK, were rebuffed and told they'd be better off on their own). That, in turn, was followed by a period of extreme economic inertia as a resurgent Germany (funded by American largesse in the form of the Marshall Plan) increasingly made inroads into British markets.

When Britain joined the EEC (as it then was) on 01 January 1973 we were commonly known on the continent as 'the sick man of Europe'. More than 70 per cent of our trade was with the EEC-8 (it's down to 47 per cent now with the EU-27); France was growing at nearly 10 per cent per annum while we were all but going backwards. We were coerced into the European project at a moment of extreme weakness.

The withering of the four pillars

My thesis is that gradually, over time, Britain's membership of the EEC-EU eroded – and has all but withered – the four pillars on which the grand social alliance that is the British Conservative Party stands. But, of course, that grand social alliance is no longer one between the landed aristocracy and the merchant class – British society has moved on and would be unrecognisable to Sir Robert Peel.

The modern Tory aristocracy is a curious aggregation of the city-dwelling (all right, *metropolitan* – meaning London-based) elite: much of the City; the CBI (which I am on record as describing as 'a lunch club for fat and lonely people'), a small *bien-pensant* corner of the BBC; a faction within the Anglican Synod; people who work for media organisations owned by Rupert Murdoch; numerous tax-exile pop stars; and (to borrow from Disraeli) the row of defunct volcanoes who pass for party elders – Sir John Major, Lord Heseltine, Sir Oliver Letwin, Ken Clarke, George Osborne.

The merchant class and its aspirant fellow-travellers are, pretty much, everyone else who hates Corbyn's Labour and, increasingly, the EU elite. (And who would rather have an appendectomy than vote Liberal Democrat, the Independent Group or the Green Party. And by the way, would only vote Ukip while wearing a gas mask). These people (with whom I identify) are finding it increasingly difficult even to engage the new Tory aristocracy at all.

The Tory corpus infected

How could the EU bacillus have infected the Tory corpus so pathologically?

First pillar. The EU is inherently anti-capitalist (and anti-American – even though France and Germany have had their defences subsidised by the USA for nearly 75 years). It is pro-regulation and instinctively pro-tax. It believes, in common with many European states, that most good things arise from state spending. It crushes entrepreneurship. It suffers from outrageous levels of unemployment because it fervidly resists a UK-style flexible labour market. It has created a currency union embracing nations with very differing economic structures thus imposing wholesale deflation on the trade deficit nations of southern Europe with massively deleterious economic and social consequences. In real terms, Italians are less well off than they were in 1999.

Second pillar. It is increasingly evident that the long-term objective of the EU elite is to create a United States of Europe (of some description) which would entirely complete the process of extinguishing national sovereignty amongst EU members, which has been in train since 1958. If I were Croatian, I would probably think this a good wheeze (though I might remember that Germany was not such a beneficent overlord in 1941-45). Being British, I cannot see any reason to throw away a thousand years of common law which has served my ancestors well in exchange for a slightly cheaper (diesel-powered!) Mercedes.

Third pillar. The EU has undermined the very notion of citizenship. A Polish worker arriving in the UK in the years after 2003 was accorded exactly the same rights and benefits as a true-born Englishman who had paid tax all his life. One reason why social mobility has seized up is that mass low-skilled immigration drove down wages at the bottom end thus forcing local-born people onto welfare and choking aspiration. Educational attainment amongst the white English working classes (especially males) has actually gone backwards. The skills gap between the haves and have-nots is still widening. Apprenticeships have declined while local-born aspirant students have to compete with foreign applicants for university places.

Fourth pillar. As for freedom and democracy – merchant Tories believe that the political class of both colours decided that it was more expedient to outsource decision-making and law-making powers to a remote supra-national bureaucracy than undertake those tasks itself. This outsourcing of sovereignty was underpinned by a surrender of judicial self-determination to a foreign court. They regard the EU as undemocratic, insensitive to public opinion, unaccountable – and often corrupt. It does not even assure rising living standards as once it did. But apparently the new Tory aristocracy doesn't see it that way.

What are the new Tories?

When Surgeon Cameron set out to operate on his patient from 2006 he did not imagine that he would end up killing him.

Since the defection of the three dysfunctional ladies to the so-called Independent Group (February 2019), thus consigning themselves to political oblivion, it has become apparent that many Tory MPs elected in

2010 are not only not capitalists but are not even patriots. One problem stems from Mr Cameron's programme to de-toxify the Conservative Party by making it a no-go zone for true-blues. (Wasn't it Mrs May who described the Tory party as The Nasty Party? – in a superb example of falling for your enemy's propaganda). When you advertise in a job description that *only nice, caring people need apply* – do not be surprised if you get a rush of second-rate applicants with no ideological lodestone except self-interest.

The A-listers parachuted in by Central Office to take safe Conservative seats in the years leading up to 2010 were overwhelmingly media-savvy, ever-emoting liberals who had never served on a neighbourhood watch, let alone done national service. The result has been effusively displayed in Mrs May's *long day's journey into night* that passed for her Brexit negotiations. They proved both spectacularly disloyal to their leader while at the same time extraordinarily confused about their strategy for the nation – apart from the necessity to remain the right side of nice (a customs union). Opposing no-deal outright was entirely illogical because that was the default outcome of not having a (despicable) Withdrawal Agreement.

One thing that we can look forward to now is an entertaining Peasant's Revolt as Conservative Constituency Associations round on the Remain-inclined MPs who made an impossible situation intractable.

Liberal democracy triumphs?

I would not take pleasure in telling Dominic Grieve MP just why I think his determination to reverse the referendum result was arrogant and wrong-headed. I know that he is a principled, scrupulous, thinking man – a gentleman – a linguist and a man of culture with a deep attachment the law. In many ways he is admirable: but he is absolutely not the future of the Tory Party; and, if ever I have the chance, I will tell him to his face that, post-Brexit, he has no place in this tribe.

When the Berlin Wall fell (1989) and then the Soviet Union dissolved overnight (Christmas 1991) it seemed that liberal democracy based on private ownership of the means of production had triumphed – once and for all. The Tories thought their claim to be *the natural party of government* had been vindicated – even though Mrs Thatcher was deposed by a pro-European cabal in November 1990. But John Major was succeeded by Tony Blair – after nearly seven years of Tory rancour over European policy.

Three things undid the Major-Blair consensus over the following two decades: the infamy of the Iraq War of 2003 and its aftermath (which the Tories supported and for which they have never apologised); the financial crisis of 2008-09 (which they have never tried to explain); and the creeping realisation, especially amongst the young, that man-made climate change is a latent menace (for which Tories have no solution). The millennials are now millenarians; as such they are very likely lost to the Tory Party. Therefore, a Tory future is uncertain.

But what has changed us most is the impact of globalism, as much in its digital as industrial forms. This has facilitated the rise of the super-rich, many of whom are trans-national. We mere merchants worry about freedom of capital (relocate to the most efficacious tax haven); and freedom of labour (a tide of economic migrants posing as refugees) – but we know that no one in power is listening.

Going back to Powell, when I think of billionaires, I *don't* smile. Yet I'm still a Tory – perhaps because I delude myself that I know what the Conservative Party is *for*.

About the contributor

Victor Hill is a financial economist, consultant, trainer and writer, with extensive experience in commercial and investment banking and fund management. His career includes stints at JP Morgan, Argyll Investment Management and World Bank IFC.

Chapter 7

Game, set and match

Conservative MPs are not acting like a political party, says Eben Black. That's why it could all be over for them

The Conservative Party has been at war with itself over Europe since at least May 1940.

As the German army rolled through France, we know Winston Churchill and his supporters wanted to fight on with the eventual aim of freeing Europe from the Nazis. Others in the party would have been quite happy to see a negotiated peace and a United Europe under Adolf Hitler, so long as Britain was guaranteed its overseas Empire.

In hindsight, you could call the appeasing Tories traitors, but they saw such a course as merely pragmatic, a way of achieving what they wanted, which was continued dominion over large parts of the earth's surface.

As far as they were concerned, France, Belgium, the Netherlands and other continental neighbours were just 'foreign' and could happily be abandoned to Hitler. India, Australia, New Zealand, swathes of Africa and half of North America were, in contrast, 'ours'.

Eurosceptics are their philosophical successors – the Empire Loyalists, the 'fog in Channel – Europe cut off' brigade, the slightly odd who would rather go to Margate than Marbella. Or they are venal, dishonest, populist politicians on the make.

How ironic then that they continually hark back to Churchill, particularly in the case of Boris Johnson, who went so far as to publish a book on Churchill in 2014 in an attempt to link his name to the great Prime Minister.

Churchill certainly believed in the Empire, and seems to have had contempt for most of its non-white inhabitants, but he knew how important Europe was and is to the UK. His views are conveniently forgotten as the Eurosceptics – among the public and in Parliament – hark back to a

'Churchillian' vision of a 1950s Britain, secure in its links to the Empire and free from interference from 'foreigners'.

Of course, none of that was ever true. Only half of the 1950s was 'Churchillian', in that he was Prime Minister from 1951 to 1955, he did not believe in this simplistic vision anyway, and it was in the course of the 1950s that the Empire began to fall apart, with even the 'white' countries demanding looser and looser links, South Africa becoming an overtly racist state and pressure mounting for independence in Africa. India had already gone, leaving minor colonial characters like the Major from *Fawlty Towers* washed up in seaside hotels.

The golden past so cherished by, I am sure, many Leave voters simply did not exist. It is at best a misapprehension and at worst a lie. But it chimes with many who lived through World War Two as children and is presented as a sunlit upland to today's disadvantaged and disgruntled who can't remember the Cold War, let alone 1939-45. It is fair to say that voters who believe in the myth are more likely to be Conservatives than not.

On the doorstep

I can't remember much about the 1960s – for reasons of age, not lifestyle – but in the minds of the public I understand Europe did not really loom large, apart from the coming of the package holiday to Spain. But politicians were waking up to the importance of the 'Common Market' on their doorstep.

Charles de Gaulle said *'non, non, non'* to Britain joining in 1963 and 1967. Large parts of the Conservative Party agreed with him, although they were also outraged that a jumped up, tin-pot foreigner who should be grateful that 'we' liberated his country from the Hun could say no to Great Britain. A remarkable feature of Conservative Euroscepticism is the ability to hold two conflicting thoughts at the same time.

I can remember the 1975 Referendum after Edward Heath took the UK into Europe in 1973. I remember my younger self, waking up to politics for the first time, being shocked at the lack of party unity, on both Labour and Tory sides. How could people of such fundamentally opposing views be in the same party? I asked myself. I would ask the same question about the Conservatives now.

The High Priest of the Little Englanders/Eurosceptics in the 1970s was, to no surprise at all, Enoch Powell, ostensibly a Conservative MP until 1974, and then, tellingly, an Ulster Unionist, who vehemently opposed Heath. Essentially these two men encapsulate the rift in the Conservative Party over Europe. Heath – urbane, a bit laissez-faire but a bit corporatist, cosmopolitan. Powell – intellectual but blinkered, determined, angry, permanently on the brink of a major explosion. Nowadays, when talking about Eurosceptics, I would of course leave out 'intellectual'.

It is no coincidence that Powell's views on Europe were accompanied by bitter opposition to immigration. It took two years from the 2016 Referendum for the media and the political class to admit that immigration from Eastern Europe had a significant bearing on the result.

I started work as a journalist in Parliament in 1988 – the beginning of the last two years of Margaret Thatcher. Eurosceptics will cite Baroness Thatcher as a leading Conservative anti-European. This, again, is utter nonsense.

I was at the Rome Summit in 1990 when she described moves to ever-closer political union as 'cloud cuckoo land', which was certainly a valid position at the time. But Margaret Thatcher was never 'anti-Europe'. She saw the value of our being in, but disagreed with parts of what it entailed. She set out to influence, or more accurately, berate, from within – and she won the UK its rebate on contributions as well as being a powerful force in the creation of the Single Market.

For the parliamentary Eurosceptics to claim to be her successors is disingenuous. They are not. Margaret Thatcher never did advocate, and never would have advocated, leaving Europe. She wanted to give the Europeans a good hand-bagging, but she knew, as the people who have led the country headlong into Brexit do not seem to, that membership is valuable and to give someone a good hand-bagging you have to be there, with your handbag.

Margaret Thatcher, at least, gave the Eurosceptics some political relief – they could express themselves without actually appearing to be challenging the Government. They could use her as a shield for their views and convince themselves that they were getting somewhere, which kept them quieter than they might otherwise have been. I suspect, however, that had Thatcher and Farage been political contemporaries, Farage might have been in line for the handbag rather than being pandered to as he was.

I bring Farage in here, not just because he was essentially the irritant which led to the June 2016 Referendum, and thus deserving of that handbag, but because he is naturally a right-wing Conservative. The only reason he is not in the party is that he is temperamentally unsuited to being in any organisation of which he is not in charge.

Why John Major was hated

Then along came John Major and the Conservative Party lid blew off. Not only did the Eurosceptics hate him because he wasn't Margaret Thatcher, but he did not appear, as she did, to share at least some of their views. I was at the Maastricht Treaty negotiations in 1992, where, in fact, moves towards 'ever closer political union' were pretty much headed off by Major, if only for the time being. The Eurosceptics did not see it like that.

Many British newspapers present used the headline the next day 'Game, Set and Match', attributing it to Major. In fact this was being bandied about – and this is an object lesson in spin – by a self-appointed 'press officer' who had once, briefly, worked for the Conservative Party but no longer did. No-one thought to ask why Major – known for his love of cricket – would use a phrase from tennis. In truth he did not say it – and if you want to know more about political spin, read my Bite-Sized book *Lies, Lobbying and Lunch*.

I was working for *The Sun,* and our headline under my by-line was 'Europe: F OFF'. Which, once you understood that F stood for 'federal', which was explained in the first paragraph, and that the word 'federal', at Major's insistence, had been taken out of the treaty creating the European Union, made sense. I can confirm that John Major did not say 'F off' either, at least on that occasion.

The Sun was at that time, and it was a brief time, vaguely in favour of Major, so we were picking out the best we could get from the Treaty which did go a long way to creating the entity which the UK voted to leave in 2016. By the time the UK crashed out of the Exchange Rate Mechanism in 1992, Major and *The Sun* were done. But the reason the crash-out happened was that Major, when Chancellor under Margaret Thatcher, had been forced to put the pound into the ERM at too high an exchange rate in order to persuade her to join. The strain of keeping the pound in, with interest rates hitting 15 per cent, nearly broke Major's government. And the country.

Major faced Eurosceptic enemies from within and without his Cabinet. Peter Lilley, Michael Portillo, John Redwood inside, people such as MPs Sir Teddy Taylor, Bill Cash, Sir Richard Body, Nick Budgen, outside.

This is not a popular view, but I believe history will portray Major as a much better Prime Minister than anyone thought at the time. Throughout his entire seven years in office he weathered constant sniping over Europe. He became the only British Prime Minister ever known to the public to have called Cabinet colleagues 'bastards'. I am sure he wasn't the first, but he was the first to be recorded saying it.

He was giving an interview in Number 10 to Michael Brunson, the then political editor of Independent Television News, when he made the remark, thinking the camera had been turned off. But it was actually still running a feed to the BBC. This, of course, caused a media storm. He did not name the "bastards" but we know he meant Portillo, Lilley and Redwood.

In Japan in the same year, 1993, he was caught on tape calling the backbench Eurosceptics 'swivel-eyed loons' and said he heard the 'flapping of white coats' whenever they approached. Major was giving a pooled, print interview to Chris Moncrieff, political editor of the Press Association, designed to go to all media outlets.

Fundamental and irresolvable

As is the way of things, every other reporter on the trip – including me – gave Moncrieff our personal mini-cassette recorders to take in with him. He set them off before Major entered the room. Major, not realising they were whirring on a mantelpiece behind him, made what he thought were off-the-record remarks. They were gleefully reported once the tapes were retrieved and listened to.

Neither of those incidents would ever happen now, unfortunately.

The Conservative split over Europe is fundamental and I think irresolvable. UKIP under Farage was merely the 'paramilitary', extremist wing of the Conservative Party, bolstered by assorted oddballs, survivalists, nearly-fascists, boorish multi-millionaires, hedge-fund managers out to make millions by shorting the pound, and people no other party would dream of entertaining as members.

The rift over Europe has caused endless damage to what we call the Conservative Party, to the extent that the situation now seems unsustainable.

I said earlier that Margaret Thatcher was not against Europe per se, but her differences of opinion with Michael Heseltine over it made a significant contribution to the enmity between them, which led to her downfall.

John Major was not brought down by Europe – although he nearly lost a confidence vote over it – but it dominated his Prime Ministership.

David Cameron had to go when he lost a referendum called by him and which his arrogance led him to believe he could not lose. The gross misjudgement of calling the referendum was, of course, designed to 'heal' the Conservatives over Europe. Well, you might say, that worked out well, Dave.

At time of writing, Theresa May – the Remainer who said 'Brexit means Brexit' without telling anybody what Brexit meant – is teetering on the edge. Three Conservative MPs have resigned from the party to join rebel Labour MPs in The Independent Group, now aiming to be an official political party with a pro-European slant.

MPs left in the Conservative Party are engaged in vicious battles over Europe, unable to agree on anything despite being in the same party. They are not acting like a party. They are not, any logic says, in the same party. They cannot all be 'Conservatives'. It could be that, for the Conservative Party as we know it, it is 'Game, Set and Match', as John Major did not say.

About the contributor

Eben Black was a national newspaper journalist for the best part of 20 years, working in Parliament. He worked for the Press Association, the national news agency supplying stories to all other media outlets, then for *The Sun, Today, News of the World* and the *Sunday Times*. He now runs EruditePR, a PR, public affairs and lobbying company.

Chapter 8

Brexit chaos, separation and economic meltdown: what keeps Scottish Tories awake at night

The Conservatives are now the second party in Scotland, says John McLellan, and will remain strong, despite Brexit, as voters understand the future of the United Kingdom is the real issue

Seven years ago the Scottish Conservative Party faced a stark choice, but the constitutional wrangling was nothing to do with Europe but everything to do with the party's ability to argue for the maintenance of the United Kingdom.

For the Scottish party the argument about Europe has not so much played second fiddle to the debate about Scotland's place in the United Kingdom, but placed it firmly as first reserve for the third violins. The battle with Scottish Nationalism comes first because its threat is the most pressing, and while differences of opinion within the ranks about Brexit are as real as they are in the South, they do not create the same tensions. Vocal dissension from Ruth Davidson's support for the Prime Minister was largely limited to outbursts from Aberdeen South MP Ross Thomson but even he came onside by the time of the third vote on the Draft Withdrawal Agreement.

The visceral hatred for Scottish Conservatism within the SNP, Green and Corbyn Labour parties has created a sense of unity and purpose that makes the Party all the more determined not to let differences of opinion on the future relationship with Europe get in the way of the duty to give a strong voice to those who do not buy into the emerging statist, high-tax, politically-correct consensus which is hardening much nearer to the centre than ever before.

In the run-up to the 1997 General Election, Labour in Scotland fought on a ticket of establishing a Scottish Parliament and Conservative opposition manifested itself in stunts like then Scottish Secretary Michael Forsyth solemnly marching up Edinburgh's Royal Mile in the ceremonial return of the Stone of Scone to Scotland from Westminster Abbey, as if handing over a Mediaeval rock would turn the electoral tide.

The reaction to the Labour landside and the two-part referendum which followed was to keep fighting against devolution and the result was again to be resoundingly defeated. When the Parliament eventually convened in 1999, the proportionate system gave a platform to the Conservative vote, which contained the rump of those Scots who felt the new institution would just be one big Labour-dominated Strathclyde Regional Council which would just find ways to fritter away voters' hard-earned cash.

Labour certainly felt its hegemony would continue as long as its partnership with the Lib Dems continued, to the extent that a senior figure like Wendy Alexander felt able to take a step back from front-line politics to develop long-term policies, because the coalition would be in power for as long as it wanted. The loss of two Labour First Minsters – first the sudden death of Donald Dewar and then the resignation of Henry McLeish – followed by the lacklustre and lackadaisical administration of Jack McConnell and the catastrophic organisation of the 2007 elections opened the door to an SNP minority by the narrowest of margins.

Minority meant caution, which gave the SNP a reputation for competence and, combined with a poor Labour campaign and collapse of the Lib Dem vote in the wake of the 2010 coalition deal with the Conservatives, the 2011 Scottish Parliament election outcome was stunning. The Lib Dem vote went straight to the Nationalists and the SNP won an absolute majority the system was supposed to prevent. Independence was not even in the SNP's top five manifesto pledges, but the result transformed a seemingly unrealisable dream into a priority.

Breakaway plans

The result also proved the good personal ratings of Scottish Conservative leader Annabel Goldie did not automatically translate into electoral support and the reins would have been handed to Murdo Fraser MSP had he not unveiled his plan to split the Scottish party from its UK parent. As well as creating a new relationship between the Scottish and UK Conservative parties along the lines of the German CDU and Bavarian SCU, he also promised to campaign for more powers for the Scottish Parliament.

Without the now unavoidable independence referendum Fraser might have won the day, but even though most of the MSP group backed him, for the Scottish party to break away at the same time as arguing against Scotland's split from the UK as a whole was seen by the national party as suicidal.

The resulting leadership election in which the unknown Ruth Davidson, only recently elected for the first time herself, won on a platform of no split and no more devolution, meant most of the parliamentary group had their faces set against the new leader from the start. When Davidson eventually accepted the Scottish Parliament had to have more responsibility for raising its own finances, open rebellion by those who felt she had been elected on a false promise was only avoided by tight management and the strength of her performances as the independence referendum campaign proper got underway in the autumn of 2013.

Ruth Davidson's reputation has only grown stronger since then; after victory in the Independence referendum, a barn-storming role in the Remain campaign in 2016, and sweeping gains in UK, Scottish and local elections, only a fool would argue the direction in which she has taken the party is wrong.

Yet in 2015 there was little clear progress, with the party still stuck on one MP in the General Election which saw David Cameron clinch a 30-seat majority. Part of the reason was the effect of the Lib Dem collapse had already been played out in Scotland and with the Scottish independence question seemingly settled, much of the anti-Labour vote could safely endorse the SNP as a party guaranteed to stand up for Scotland if nothing else.

Corbyn and Brexit change the game

What changed everything was Jeremy Corbyn and Brexit. With Labour no longer a safe centre-ground option and the Lib Dems still irrelevant, the only place for a Unionist vote was the new, acceptable face of liberal capitalism in Ruth Davidson's Conservatives. By immediately seizing the 2016 EU Referendum result as an opportunity to grasp the 62 per cent of Scots who voted Remain, First Minister Nicola Sturgeon reignited the independence campaign but made two significant miscalculations.

Firstly , she failed to recognise that Unionists who voted Remain did not suddenly become Nationalists because the UK voted to Leave; people who recognised that while leaving Europe might be regrettable, with Scotland trading four times as much with the rest of the UK as the EU then breaking the Union would be a far greater act of self-harm.

But perhaps more importantly, she underestimated how many SNP voters were Leavers – some 400,000 of them. These were people as opposed to any control from Brussels as they were from London and saw Brexit as a way of breaking one bond with plenty of time to cut the other.

In the North-East Scotland constituencies, where agriculture and fisheries are central to both the economy and regional identity, Brexit promised freedom from the hated EU Common Fisheries Policy while mismanagement of farming subsidies further undermined confidence in the SNP as a party of competent government. The result in the 2017 snap general election was defeat in previously solid seats like Moray and Gordon where deputy leader Angus Robertson and ex-leader Alex Salmond were ousted, and the Scottish Conservatives went from one seat to 13.

From a position in 2015 when Ruth Davidson's popularity was thought by some to be echoing that of her predecessor by failing to deliver real electoral gains, by mid-2017 the party had become the second force in Scottish politics. Despite the chaos of the EU withdrawal and attacks on domestic policies like the Universal Credit roll-out, there is little sign of that changing. Indeed if anything the party's position is potentially stronger as the SNP-Green budget accord promises to deliver higher taxation with only the Conservatives able to mount effective counter-arguments.

The UK is the key objective

It is true there are some on the outer fringes of the party who could chose a different path depending on the outcome of the Brexit process, but the vast majority of members recognise the course set by both Ruth Davidson and Scottish Secretary David Mundell domestically delivers far greater clarity of purpose as far as the key objective of holding the United Kingdom together is concerned.

Most in the Scottish Party (maybe there are one or two who don't) also accepted that while a no-deal departure could be devastating, it was essential it stayed on the negotiating table because the devastation would not be one-sided. So too is there recognition the absolute intransigence of the Democratic Unionists poses a threat to the very Union both they and the Scottish Conservatives exist to protect.

If there has been one small crumb of comfort from the agonies the UK Government has faced in delivering on the 2016 result it has been to provide the best illustration possible of the problems with which an independent Scotland heading back into the EU would be confronted.

If it's hard to leave the Customs Union and maintain a frictionless border between Northern Ireland and the Republic it will be the same for Scotland and England. And if it takes years to untangle a political arrangement which has been in existence for a couple of decades, how long will it take to unravel one which is more than 300 years old?

That's before an independent Scottish Government works out how it will cover a taxation deficit of more than £13bn (£1,576 per head) when it has no credit record, or works out what currency it would use when continuing to use the pound on anything other than an unofficial basis would be rejected by London without some sort of fiscal control. That would defeat the purpose of independence, while the Euro is another reason those 400,000 SNP voters want nothing to do with the EU.

The answer is a new Scottish currency which, as it did in 2014, will again scare the Bejaysus out of most voters. And with that £13bn deficit, no credit history and a tax-and-spend approach to the economy, it would be as attractive to the money markets as Zimbabwe dollars or Venezuelan Bolivares. The old Alex Salmond adage of 'no country ever got poor by having oil' is being shown to be the nonsense it always was with every day that passes in Venezuela.

But Scottish Conservatives are not so naïve as to think the numbers alone will be enough to win the arguments. The debate must be had and the assertions of the hardening left challenged, otherwise the financial never-never land of parties like the Greens who regard economic growth itself as an existential threat to the planet, and with whom the SNP are happy to do business, will hold sway.

The same divisions of opinion which threaten the party in the South exist in Scotland, but the difference is Scottish Conservatives understand that schism only hands opportunity to the Unicorn chasers in the other parties. The result in council groups like mine, with 17 members, is we acknowledge differences of opinion but don't dwell on them. Of much more urgency is our position on local taxation and service delivery, and keeping Nationalism in its box, so why waste our time and energy on matters which risk division and we can't control anyway?

Scotland has been in a perpetual political campaign ever since 2011 and the divisions created by Brexit seem tame compared to the increasing bitterness experienced in the run-up to 2014 and beyond. It is also why Scottish Conservatives are united against the so-called 'People's Vote' because the precedent it could set for re-opening 2014's decisive result. Have those Southern Conservatives backing a re-run considered a second vote to leave the EU could trigger a second vote to leave the UK? We are confident we would win again because support for independence has not shifted despite everything, but why should we have to?

The defeats of the Withdrawal Agreement are playing into the SNP's hands and in the event of a Norway style free trade agreement they will waste no time in arguing than independence is just a short hop away.

In a country where most economic indicators continue to lag behind the rest of the UK and the burden of taxation is only upwards – higher income tax, higher property transaction tax, and more taxes on tourists and cars on the way – the idea that more of this and breaking up Britain at the same time will somehow make us all better off is what really keeps Scottish Conservatives awake in the middle of the night. For us, Brexit chaos could just be for starters.

About the contributor

John McLellan has been a City of Edinburgh Conservative councillor since 2017 and was Director of Communications for the Scottish Conservatives in 2012-13. He has edited *The Scotsman,* the *Edinburgh Evening News* and *Scotland on Sunday* and is currently Director of the Scottish Newspaper Society.

Chapter 9

There may be some wilderness years, but the Tories will survive

Current divisions are not helpful, and previous internal battles were disastrous, says Nicholas Stone, but the Conservative Party will always bounce back

> *"If the Prime Minister wanted to get Chequers through, she'd be dependent on socialist votes"*
> – Jacob Rees-Mogg, Conservative MP, Chair – European Research Group, July 2018

Despite open divisions, the unfolding Brexit crisis has largely demonstrated that the Conservatives prioritise party unity over national interest.

Current prime minister Theresa May has been a lifelong Conservative. She won't want to be remembered as the Conservative leader whose Brexit divided the party she leads. However she does lead a party which is struggling to coalesce around an agreed policy on the future relationship with the Europe.

On her right, is the ruthless European Research Group (ERG) of around 90 MPs who are indifferent to party unity except on their own terms. While on her left are more sympathetic party grouping who yearn for a closer economic relationship with the Europe.

On Brexit, Mrs May has generally tacked to the right and the ERG. Her preferred Brexit vision laid out in her 2017 Lancaster House speech and a series of Commons amendments since have aimed to appease the wing more wanting to press for the most abrupt form of Brexit. This was illustrated when more than 100 of her own parliamentary party rejected the Government's negotiated Withdrawal Agreement. While she initially made cross-party overtures, ultimately it was ERG demands over the backstop which has directed Mrs May's course of action. In other words, party unity remains the prize.

Past party divisions

Brexit could be symptomatic of periodic Conservative convulsions over trade policy. Other Conservative Party crises led to damaging political ruptures.

The protectionist Corn Laws divided the country in the 1840s. The Corn Laws were tariffs and trade restrictions and became a growing source of opposition among urban groups. Land-owning Conservatives represented the obstacle to the repeal of the Corn Laws.

Indeed supporters included banker James Wilson, who advanced the abolition of the Corn Laws with the launch of his newspaper *The Economist*. Irish famine provided fresh impetus for Conservative prime minster Robert Peel to call for the Corn Laws' repeal, despite opposition in his own party.

Mr Peel was able to pass the law repealing the Corn Laws but only with support of the opposition Whig MPs. As a result, Mr Peel resigned as a Conservative prime minister. But there were other consequences. With the support of other like-minded free-trade Conservatives, the Whigs transformed into the Liberal Party.

Less than six years in to the 20th century, Conservative prime minister Arthur Balfour was to face cabinet splits. And the issue was again tariffs, which split his cabinet between those who preferred free trade and those who wanted tariff reform.

Mr Balfour attempted a political fudge, with retaliatory tariffs to punish others. The cabinet split, resignations followed, and Mr Balfour himself resigned in December 1905. In the election which followed, the Conservatives were routed and even Mr Balfour lost his seat. The Liberals were swept to power with a landslide victory and a majority of more than 120 seats. It was to be last the time the Liberals won a general election outright.

But in both the cases of Peel and Balfour ending their careers, the Conservative had survived as a nationwide political party. When he became party leader in 2005, David Cameron wanted to stop his party 'banging on about Europe'. He failed. And it's at this point we need to introduce the European Research Group.

The rise of the European Research Group

Conservative MP Sir Michael Spicer formed the European Research Group (ERG) in 1993 in response to growing concerns of Maastricht Treaty European Union political integration.

Over the next two decades, the ERG has taken control of the governing Conservative policy. The ERG supporters are strong and ruthless enough to ensure the Conservative unity is preserved on their terms. Both Mr Cameron and now Mrs May attaches importance to maintain party unity and so struggles to face down the ERG. By contrast, the pro-EU moderates prioritise party unity over their own Brexit interests.

The ERG is a private (third-party) organisation and thus not accountable to the taxpayers funding it. As a private (third-party) organisation, the ERG does not have to publish a list of its members. For these reasons, the ERG does not have to communicate their accounts and itemised spending. The ERG receives public funds through recorded taxpayer-funded expense claims made by MPs. It also receives private donations. Expenditures claimed by MPs are reviewed by the Independent Parliamentary Standards Authority.

At the time of writing, the ERG is chaired by Jacob Rees-Mogg MP. Other current and former ERG members include current and former members of the ERG include Michael Gove, Iain Duncan Smith, Liam Fox, Chris Grayling, Priti Patel, John Whittingdale, Ann-Marie Trevelyan, Bernard Jenkin, Steve Baker and Douglas Carswell.

Six steps to a hard Brexit

Since Mr Cameron became leader in 2005, the Conservative have party have undergone a considerable shift to an anti-EU ideology. Less than 10 years ago, the party was committed to membership of the European Union and all its institutions including the Customs Union and Single Market . Now the UK government has active option of leaving the European Union without any trading agreements whatsoever.

There are six steps that moved the Conservative party from mainstream to a hard Brexit:

1. Taking the Conservative party out of the European People's Party

Fearing that he was failing to shore up support on the right of the party, back in 2005, Mr Cameron pledged that as leader he would withdraw his MEPs from the centre-right EPP-ED grouping in the European . With the support of other parties across Eastern Europe, the Conservative Party established the European Conservatives and Reforms. This is a transnational European parliamentary group which includes not just the Conservatives by the far-right Swedish Democrats and the governing PiS Law and Justice party in Poland.

2. An EU membership referendum

Back in 2010, a group of right-wing Conservative backbenchers saw the potential for the newly created Backbench Business Committee. As hard line Brexiteer Peter Bone MP said: "If we hadn't had the Backbench Business Committee, I don't think the Referendum would have happened.". Events in October 2011 were to prove pivotal.

An opportunity for backbench debate appeared and one of the groups – Philip Hollobone – put down a Brexit referendum. To motivate support among the group of Brexiteers, Steve Baker (future Brexit minister), circulated a briefing. Mr Baker's briefing said "..in every constituency, voters are signing the People's Pledge, promising to support candidates who give them an In/Out referendum..".

More Conservative MPs were emboldened.

Mr Cameron's government countered Mr Hollobone's motion by declaring a three-line whip against it and also rescheduled the debate from a Thursday backwater to a prime-time afternoon slot. Foreign Secretary William Hague tried to quell the rebellion by calling the motion 'a piece of graffiti'. In the end, the Government won the motion, but 81 Conservative MPs defied the party whip.

Despite the defeat, the group of Brexiteers kept up their pressure on Mr Cameron's government. Next nearly 100 Conservative MPs signed a letter backing the idea of referendum – the thought being that while the Liberal Democrats and Labour might vote down a referendum bill, they would put themselves firmly on the wrong side of public opinion in the process, while the Conservatives would give themselves an edge on Ukip, especially with the May 2015 general election looming.

By January 2013, Mr Cameron announced that Conservative party policy was to hold a referendum. By February 2016, he called it. The date for the Referendum was 23 June 2016

3. Conservative government policy UK leave the EU

Mr Cameron did not want to implement the results of the Referendum. He resigned. But following the peculiar, incomplete leadership contest, Mr Cameron was replaced with someone who was going to implement the Referendum: Theresa May.

Having benefited from the wider political crisis Mrs May's sole reason for becoming Prime Minister was to implement Brexit. She sacked Remain-supporting George Osborne. And she appointed three Brexit supporters – Liam Fox, David Davies and Boris Johnson – to three key cabinet ministerial positions. Two created for the purpose of Brexit and a third was foreign affairs.

4. Demand red lines and trigger Article 50

Once installed as the new Conservative leader, the hard-line Conservative Brexiteers were able to vocalise their demands. Encourage by some in the print press, and keen to impress recently empowered voters, the policy became the hardest Brexit possible. There was no discussion on compromises on the Single Market or the Customs Union. This policy was formulated at the Birmingham October 2016 Conservative party.

It was at the conference that Mrs May announced a deadline for Article 50. In so doing, she then formalised that the day of Brexit would be on or before 31 March 2019. These party conference announcements were adopted as UK government policy, at Mrs May's January 2017 Lancaster House speech. It was also there that she confirmed that the UK could leave the EU without a deal, if she did not get what she wanted. The no-deal Brexit option was later included in the Conservative party manifesto at the June 2017 election.

Mrs May's decision to include the no-deal Brexit as an option may have been her single biggest strategic mistake. It has been adopted by the

Conservatives' ERG group as their mantra, driving a coach and horses through any policy detail, emboldened voters who can chant 'walk away' and normalised the debate of leaving without a deal.

5. Demanded rejection of the Brexit deal

After 18 months of negotiations, the Brexit deal was rejected in a record parliamentary defeat. Almost the only MPs to vote for the deal were ministers, their juniors and assistants: Mrs May's ministerial payroll. Less than a month later, in order to buy time and please the ERG, the UK government voted for amendment which rejected the agreed deal's Northern Ireland backstop. The Government had rejected the very Brexit deal it had negotiated and signed off just three months earlier.

6. Demand the no-deal Brexit

Many in the Conservative party now demand a no-deal Brexit — the most abrupt departure from the EU and the most instant change in the UK's trading circumstances. No transition period, no Customs Union, no Single Market, no trade deals. And all at the stroke of 23:00 on Friday 29 March 2019 (or whenever!). But this preferred version of Brexit is branded as WTO Brexit, Clean Brexit or Global Brexit. But it amounts to the same thing: leaving without a Withdrawal Agreement.

The outlook

As at February 2019, the UK political situation is volatile. Predictions are difficult. Nevertheless, there are some useful points.

If the Brexit withdrawal agreement is implemented, the UK enters a standstill transition period. Expected to last until 31 December 2022, the UK government renegotiates its relationship with the EU. During this transition period, the Conservative will be choosing a new leader. That means a new Conservative prime minister going to Brussels to continue talk.

We have seen the Conservative has survived previous divisive policies. The Corn Laws, tariff reforms and — famously — the Conservative Party dumped Margaret Thatcher — so they could then dump the increasingly unpopular Poll Tax.

Conservative Party survival currently appears to allow not just disunity in the parliamentary group, but also in government itself. Cabinet ministers have gone on the record opposing Mrs May's approach to the no-deal Brexit strategy, yet have not been sacked; a clear breach of collective cabinet responsibility.

The Conservative party will survive Brexit. Some MPs will defect to new groups, others will compromise their own positions. The disorientating domestic effects of Brexit may lead to a general election defeat and a period in the political wilderness for the Conservatives.

About the contributor

Nicholas Stone has an interest in politics and economic going back to school days. He studied economics and politics from 1983 to 1988, all the way to degree level. UK politics have always featured heavily in his interests and studies. The demise of Margaret Thatcher, the 1909-11 House of Lords reforms and the rise of the European Research Group have all been studied.

He travels widely across Europe. Only three EU member states (Latvia, Lithuania and Cyprus) still remain to be visited.

Chapter 10

History will not look kindly on Mrs May

The Prime Minister's legacy will not command much respect in the years ahead, says Liz Gerard

The Prime Minister affects the persona of a gawky school prefect with the best of intentions, doing her duty as a vicar's daughter should, a woman so brought up on the path of righteousness that the naughtiest thing she can remember doing is running through a field of wheat.

Maybe she forgot that she created a 'hostile environment' for immigrants, those racist vans that went round housing estates telling people to 'go home', urging neighbour to inform on 'foreign' neighbour. Maybe she forgot that little fiction about the man whose human rights all came down to having a pet cat.

History will not look kindly on Mrs May.

Yes, she took on an impossible job. But, as the woman in the yellow jacket on Question Time so eloquently put it a few weeks back, it's time we stopped feeling sorry for Mrs May. Mrs May is where she is because that's where she wanted to be.

Nobody dragged her through the door of No 10 like a medieval Speaker to the Commons chair. She volunteered for it. She wanted it as much as Boris Johnson wants it. She admitted in that cosy tv sofa interview about Philip putting out the bins that she'd had her eyes on Downing Street when she was in Cameron's shadow cabinet in the early years of the century. So for at least a decade – and possibly two.

Once she was in, she tried to emulate the most successful Prime Minister of the past generation in governing by soundbite. Brexit means Brexit. Strong and stable. Delivering on the will of the people.

Except that Mr Blair was able to walk and chew gum. Mrs May seems incapable of either.

He prosecuted an ill-advised (many would say illegal) war, but he did manage to run the country and keep his party united at the same time. He recognised that there were domestic policies that also required his attention. Mrs May is a one-trick pony and she can't even pull that one off. She has done absolutely nothing during her tenure other than fail to deliver Brexit and continue the destruction of her party.

What she said

When she first stood at that lectern in Downing Street, she set out how she would bring the country together – by promising to give 17m people what they had asked for and effectively telling the rest of the country to suck it up.

Then she appointed a team of charlatans and incompetents to the key jobs and when they proved unequal to their tasks – as they did to a man – she didn't sack them: they sacked themselves. Because they could see that she was even more hopeless than they were.

She said she wouldn't hold an election to legitimise her position. Then she decided she would. To get rid of the 'saboteur' Remainer MPs standing in her way and secure a landslide majority. Her big selling point was that she was a strong leader. But voters could see that she was no more than the designated driver on a charabanc outing, trying to stay sober while the uncontrolled and uncontrollable drunks in the back of the coach larked about, shouting conflicting instructions on which road to take. It did not turn out well.

She spent millions fighting court cases to stop any counter view being heard – first to stop MPs having any say on Brexit, then to stop a QC establishing whether Britain could revoke Article 50 if it wanted. Not to suggest that she do so, simply to find out whether it was possible. That did not turn out well for Mrs May either.

She said MPs would have a meaningful vote on the deal that she had negotiated with the EU in December and that the vote would not be delayed. She first tried to render it meaningless and then, facing certain defeat at the hands of her own party, she delayed.

In the meantime, having survived an attempted leadership coup but still unable to convince her MPs to back her version of Brexit, she spent more of our money touring the country and placing ads in social media to persuade 'the people' that her deal was a good deal. The very people she was adamant should not have another say on that or any other deal.

In the Commons, though, her plan went down to a record defeat and she was forced to accept that the next time MPs had a vote on Brexit it really would mean something. Then she brought it back and lost again – and brought it back again and lost again, proving that, to her at least, MPs' votes meant nothing.

History will not look kindly on Mrs May.

In trying to sell what she insisted was the best possible withdrawal agreement, she had emphasised three key advantages.

The first was that it would mean an end to freedom of movement.

Most regard 'freedom' as a good thing, but in her book it is bad. Even, apparently, for British people who would lose just as many rights to live and work where they choose as the Europeans she wants to keep out of the country.

The contribution of immigrants

In pandering to the anti-immigration lobby, she neglected to mention that more immigrants come from outside the EU than within it. She neglected to mention that European immigrants make a greater contribution to the British economy than the native population (they tend to be young, fit workers who pay taxes and don't need educating or old-age care).

Meanwhile immigrants from outside Europe, particularly the Commonwealth – whose admission is entirely in the hands of the government – cost us money (which is not to say they don't enrich society in other ways). But she didn't mention that. Or dwell on the fact that countries such as India are already demanding that more visas be issued in exchange for a trade deal.

And, most of all, she glossed over the fact that it is possible to restrict immigration even from the EU. It's just that Britain has chosen not to use the tools at its disposal. And she never, ever acknowledged who had been in charge of immigration policy – including the Windrush scandal – for the first six years of the Conservative government: one T. May.

The second advantage of her deal was that it would mean an end to the jurisdiction of the European Court of Justice, a court with a nasty habit of upholding British courts' rulings on the implementation of British laws, often against the Government. Mrs May hates the European Court of Human Rights even more, but that isn't the same thing at all. It isn't even linked to the EU. But she doesn't labour that point. Easier to let people think what they will and not put them right. We can disentangle ourselves from that one another day.

The third advantage was that it would protect the fishing industry. As an island state, we have a sentimental attachment to anyone with anything to do with the sea. We instinctively know that the fishing industry is important – but do we know how many people it employs?

About 12,000, a sixth of them part-timers. Mrs May took pride in protecting the livelihoods of 10,000 full-time workers.

Excellent. But what of other industries? What of the 200,000 jobs already lost as a result of Brexit? She listened to the fishing lobby (dominated by five rich families) but not, apparently to Jaguar Land Rover or to Airbus or to the City or to the creative industry. And she didn't seem to find anything odd about pro-Brexit campaigner James Dyson moving his 'British' business to Singapore.

What she didn't notice

But as much as she cried 'Look over there!' with her three big 'wins', her MPs – and the Democratic Unionists she depended on to stay in office – insisted on looking over here: at the Irish border, at the fact that Britain would remain in the Customs Union for the foreseeable future, at the fact that we'd have all the costs and restrictions of EU membership with none of the benefits. And they didn't like what they saw.

History will not look kindly on Mrs May.

She said she wanted to create a fairer society and – wearing a £1,000 pair of leather trousers – denounced the Remainer 'elites' who didn't understand the privations of the Just About Managings. Yet she did not notice that the most vocal Brexiteers were millionaires and disaster capitalists who were busy shorting the pound and applying for foreign passports.

She promised to bring the country together, but instead she reinforced its divisions by focusing on the 17m and refusing to acknowledge, let alone listen to, the other 30m voters. Just as she tried to placate 40-odd hardline

Tory Brexiteers and a handful of Democratic Unionists, while trying to sideline the other 600 MPs – including a majority from her own party, which is now more riven than ever.

David Cameron called the Referendum to try to sort out internal problems in the Conservative party. When it went wrong, he went whistling down the road, leaving others to deal with the mess. Mrs May was only too pleased to take on the task. But instead of healing the divisions, she has presided over the disintegration of her party.

Having opted for Remain (although her campaigning was as half-hearted as Jeremy Corbyn's), Mrs May ~~immediately~~ switched sides ~~once~~ the moment the keys to No 10 were on the table and went at Brexit with all the vigour of a new convert. Her way was the only way and counter views from any quarter – most particularly less fickle pro-European colleagues – were not welcome.

When a rabid Brexit Press started labelling Tory backbenchers unpatriotic 'Remoaners', 'traitors', 'saboteurs' and 'mutineers', she did nothing to defend their right to speak and still less to address their concerns.

Just as she had sided with the *Daily Mail* over the judiciary after that 'Enemies of the people' front page, so she was happy to allow it and the *Telegraph* to turn their fire on her own MPs. She seemed to regard them not as colleagues to be nurtured and respected, but as lobby fodder who should just shut up and do as they were told.

For more than two years, the woman who had once cautioned that the Conservatives were seen as the nasty party, sat back and watched as the nastiness spread through the party, the media, the country.

When it turned to aggression, with attacks on Europeans who had lived in the country for years, she did nothing. When her own MPs were abused and threatened outside Parliament, she said nothing. Rather she was happy to allow talk of civil unrest, rioting, the rise of the fascist Right – even martial law – to be thrown into the mix of awful things that would happen if she didn't get her way.

This from the leader of a party that had faced down the IRA and terrorists of all suits; the party that had the mantra of not giving in to threats of violence. Now its senior members were peddling such threats on prime-time TV – and she said or did nothing to counter their view.

The *Mail*, the *Express*, the *Sun* and the *Telegraph* were her friends and spiritual guides. With them on her side, nothing could stop her.

Except that hardly anyone else was on her side. And now even the once-devoted Tory Press is split: half of them desperately backing her deal as the least worst option, the others pushing for Mogg and Johnson's hard Brexit.

Where do they go?

Everyone knows that Mrs May is an incompetent leader who will be junked at the earliest opportunity, but could anyone rescue the party? If almost anyone but Jeremy Corbyn were leader of the Labour party, the Tories would surely be out for a generation – possibly forever.

So where do they go from here? There is much talk of a new party and there are certainly millions in the centre who feel they have no political voice.

Could Tory and Labour Remainers come together to provide one? The omens are not promising. The SDP looked a shoo-in last time voters faced this void in the Thatcher-Foot era, but the revolution fizzled out, the party merged with the Liberals and still made no progress.

The Liberal Democrats should have been the obvious vote for Remainers in the 2017 election, but they got nowhere. The Tiggers – or Change UK – stirred up a brief storm, but have so far failed to secure the further defections they might have hoped for. It's hard to see the likes of Ken Clarke and Yvette Cooper abandoning their lifetime political homes to gamble on a brave new world in cahoots with either set. Not least because the independents and the LibDems have yet to get together.

If a new party is to emerge, maybe it's more likely to crystallise from the Right. With Ukip turning more rightwards, there is space at that end of the spectrum.

Could Rees-Mogg team up with Farage and steal the populist Tory vote? Would Boris Johnson see such a hybrid as his opportunity at last to seize the big prize, leaving the 'wet' one-nation Tories to nurse what's left of their party?

It could be the saving of the Conservatives. It might even make them re-electable. But only if the Leave/Brexit culprits – Johnson, Fox, Gove, Davies et al – were prepared to take their chances in the Moggites' brave new world. If they insisted on staying put, which they almost certainly would, there's no hope.

When Mrs May came to power, the nation was smouldering over the Referendum. She could have tried the foam canister, but opted instead for the petrol can. She may yet pull a charred and mangled Brexit out of the fire. But the country and her party will burn for years.

History will not look kindly on Mrs May.

About the contributor

Liz Gerard worked for *The Times* for more than 30 years, latterly as night editor and business night editor. She now edits the journalism website SubScribe.

Bite-Sized Public Affairs Books are designed to provide insights and stimulating ideas that affect us all in, for example, journalism, social policy, education, government and politics.

They are deliberately short, easy to read, and authoritative books written by people who are either on the front line or who are informed observers. They are designed to stimulate discussion, thought and innovation in all areas of public affairs. They are all firmly based on personal experience and direct involvement and engagement.

The most successful people all share an ability to focus on what really matters, keeping things simple and understandable. When we are faced with a new challenge most of us need quick guidance on what matters most, from people who have been there before and who can show us where to start. As Stephen Covey famously said, "The main thing is to keep the main thing, the main thing."

But what exactly is the main thing?

Bite-Sized books were conceived to help answer precisely that question crisply and quickly and, of course, be engaging to read, written by people who are experienced and successful in their field.

The brief? Distil the 'main things' into a book that can be read by an intelligent non-expert comfortably in around 60 minutes. Make sure the book enables the reader with specific tools, ideas and plenty of examples drawn from real life. Be a virtual mentor.

We have avoided jargon – or explained it where we have used it as a shorthand – and made few assumptions about the reader, except that they are literate and numerate, involved in understanding social policy, and that they can adapt and use what we suggest to suit their own, individual purposes. Most of all the books are focused on understanding and exploiting the changes that we witness every day but which come at us in what seems an incoherent stream.

They can be read straight through at one easy sitting and then referred to as necessary – a trusted repository of hard-won experience.

Bite-Sized Books Catalogue

Business Books

Ian Benn
Write to Win
How to Produce Winning Proposals and RFP Responses

Matthew T Brown
Understand Your Organisation
An Introduction to Enterprise Architecture Modelling

David Cotton
Rethinking Leadership
Collaborative Leadership for Millennials and Beyond

Richard Cribb
IT Outsourcing: 11 Short Steps to Success
An Insider's View

Phil Davies
How to Survive and Thrive as a Project Manager
The Guide for Successful Project Managers

Paul Davies
Developing a Business Case
Making a Persuasive Argument out of Your Numbers

Paul Davies
Developing a Business Plan
Making a Persuasive Plan for Your Business

Paul Davies
Contract Management for Non-Specialists

Paul Davies
Developing Personal Effectiveness in Business

Paul Davies
A More Effective Sales Team
Sales Management Focused on Sales People

Maiqi Ma
> Win with China
>> Acclimatisation for Mutual Success Doing Business with China

Elena Mihajloska
> Bridging the Virtual Gap
>> Building Unity and Trust in Remote Teams

Rob Morley
> Agile in Business
>> A Guide for Company Leadership

Gillian Perry
> Managing the People Side of Change
>> Ten Short Steps to Success in IT Outsourcing

Saibal Sen
> Next Generation Service Management
>> An Analytics Driven Approach

Don Sharp
> Nothing Happens Until You Sell Something
>> A Personal View of Selling Techniques

Christopher Hosford
> Great Business Meetings! Greater Business Results
>> Transforming Boring Time-Wasters into Dynamic Productivity Engines

Lifestyle Books

Anna Corthout
> Alive Again
>> My Journey to Recovery

Phil Davies
> Don't Worry Be Happy
>> A Personal Journey

Phil Davies
> Feel the Fear and Pack Anyway
>> Around the World in 284 Days

Stuart Haining
> My Other Car is an Aston
>> A Practical Guide to Ownership and Other Excuses to Quit Work and Start a Business

Bill Heine
    Cancer – Living Behind Enemy Lines Without a Map
Regina Kerschbaumer
    Yoga Coffee and a Glass of Wine
        A Yoga Journey
Gillian Perry
    Capturing the Celestial Lights
        A Practical Guide to Imagining the Northern Lights
Arthur Worrell
    A Grandfather's Story
        Arthur Worrell's War

Public Affairs Books

Eben Black
    Lies Lunch and Lobbying
        PR, Public Affairs and Political Engagement – A Guide
John Mair and Richard Keeble (Editors)
    Investigative Journalism Today:
        Speaking Truth to Power
John Mair, Richard Keeble and Farrukh Dhondy (Editors)
    V.S Naipaul:
        The legacy
Christian Wolmar
    Wolmar for London
        Creating a Grassroots Campaign in a Digital Age
John Mair and Neil Fowler (Editors)
    Do They Mean Us – Brexit Book 1
        The Foreign Correspondents' View of the British Brexit
John Mair, Alex De Ruyter and Neil Fowler (Editors)
    The Case for Brexit – Brexit Book 2
David Bailey, John Mair and Neil Fowler (Editors)
    Keeping the Wheels on the Road – Brexit Book 3
        UK Auto Post Brexit
Paul Davies, John Mair and Neil Fowler
    Will the Tory Party Ever Be the Same? – Brexit Book 4
        The Effect of Brexit
Kohn Mair and Neil Fowler (Editors)
    Oil Dorado
        Guyana's Black Gold

Fiction

Paul Davies
> The Ways We Live Now
>> Civil Service Corruption, Wilful Blindness, Commercial Fraud, and Personal Greed – a Novel of Our Times

Paul Davies
> Coming To
>> A Novel of Self-Realisation

Children's Books

Chris Reeve – illustrations by Mike Tingle
> The Dictionary Boy
>> A Salutary Tale

Fredrik Payedar
> The Spirit of Chaos
>> It Begins

Printed in Great Britain
by Amazon